ADVANCE PRAISE FOR
DESIGNING WORSHIP TOGETHER

"*Designing Worship Together: Models and Strategies for Worship Planning* goes beyond a cookie-cutter approach to worship planning and leading and provides excellent guidance based on a variety of experiences. Vanderwell and deWaal Malefyt continually challenge readers to think theologically and act scripturally, and to open themselves to Spirit-driven newness."

—HAROLD M. BEST
former dean of the Conservatory of Music,
Wheaton College

"This book gives worship planners solid biblical and theological foundations for their work. It also provides comprehensive and practical advice for congregations who truly want their worship to be as meaningful and God-glorifying as possible. Howard and Norma make clear that planning engaging, God-glorifying worship, week after week, is hard work. They also give congregations the resources needed to do that hard work."

—DUANE KELDERMAN
vice-president for administration,
Calvin Theological Seminary

"This theologically sound and practically grounded book is a rich resource for those already working together to plan worship. It will be an eye opener for those yet to implement a collaborative approach to the art of worship planning."

—JOHN FERGUSON
St. Olaf College

"The authors have spent years in dynamic collaboration and now share the fruit of their work. The result is deeply insightful, winsome, and, above all, just plain helpful."

—CORNELIUS PLANTINGA, JR.
president, Calvin Theological Seminary

"This carefully researched body of theory, method, and practice points to the very best practices to which we all could aspire. Broad in the traditions and voices it surveys, the insights found here translate across a broad spectrum of worship. This resource needs to be on the shelves of all teachers and practitioners of worship."

—TIMOTHY L. CARSON
author of *So You're Thinking About Contemporary Worship*

The Vital Worship, Healthy Congregations Series

John D. Witvliet, Series Editor

Published by the Alban Institute in Cooperation with the
Calvin Institute of Christian Worship

BOOKS PUBLISHED

C. Michael Hawn
One Bread, One Body:
Exploring Cultural Diversity in Worship

Norma deWaal Malefyt and Howard Vanderwell
Designing Worship Together:
Models and Strategies for Worship Planning

COMING SOON

Craig A. Satterlee
When God Speaks through Change:
Preaching in Times of Congregational Transition

Designing Worship Together

MODELS AND STRATEGIES FOR WORSHIP PLANNING

Norma deWaal Malefyt
Howard Vanderwell

Foreword by
Robert Webber

THE ALBAN INSTITUTE

Herndon, Virginia
www.alban.org

The Alban Institute, 2121 Cooperative Way, Suite 100, Herndon, VA 20171

Scripture quotations, unless otherwise noted, are from the New International Version of the Bible, copyright © 1973, 1978, 1984. Used by permission of Zondervan Bible Publishers.

Cover and text design by Keith McCormick and Katty Montenegro Sakoto

Cover illustration by Tacoumba Aiken.

Library of Congress Cataloging-in-Publication Data

Vanderwell, Howard.
  Designing worship together : models and strategies for worship planning /
Howard Vanderwell and Norma de Waal Malefyt ; foreword by Robert Webber.
      p. cm. — (Vital worship, healthy congregations)
  Includes bibliographical references.
  ISBN 1-56699-296-6
  1. Public worship—Planning. I. De Waal Malefyt, Norma. II. Title. III. Series.

  BV15.V36 2004
  264—dc22
                        2004022114

      09 08 07 06   VG   2 3 4 5

CONTENTS

EDITOR'S FOREWORD

HEALTHY CONGREGATIONS

Christianity is a "first-person plural" religion, where communal worship, service, fellowship, and learning are indispensable for grounding and forming individual faith. The strength of Christianity in North America depends on the presence of healthy, spiritually nourishing, well-functioning congregations. Congregations are the cradle of Christian faith, the communities in which children of all ages are supported, encouraged, and formed for lives of service. Congregations are the habitat in which the practices of the Christian life can flourish.

As living organisms, congregations are by definition in a constant state of change. Whether the changes are in membership, pastoral leadership, lay leadership, the needs of the community, or the broader culture, a crucial mark of healthy congregations is their ability to deal creatively and positively with change. The fast pace of change in contemporary culture, with its bias toward, not against change, only makes the challenge of negotiating change all the more pressing for congregations.

VITAL WORSHIP

At the center of many discussions about change in churches today is the topic of worship. This is not surprising, for worship is at the center of congregational life. To "go to church" means, for most members of congregations, "to go to worship." In *How Do We Worship?*, Mark Chaves begins his analysis with the simple assertion, "Worship is the most central and public activity engaged in by American religious congregations" (Alban Institute, 1999, p. 1). Worship styles are one of the most significant reasons that people choose to join a given congregation. Correspondingly, they are central to the identity of most congregations.

Worship is also central on a much deeper level. Worship is the locus of what several Christian traditions identify as the nourishing center of congregation life: preaching, common prayer, and the celebration of ordinances or sacraments. Significantly, what many traditions elevate to the status of "the means of grace" or even the "marks of the church" are essentially liturgical actions. Worship is central, most significantly, for theological reasons. Worship both reflects and shapes a community's faith. It expresses a congregation's view of God and enacts a congregation's relationship with God and each other.

We can identify several specific factors that contribute to spiritually vital worship and thereby strengthen congregational life.

- Congregations, and the leaders that serve them, need a shared vision for worship that is grounded in more than personal aesthetic tastes. This vision must draw on the deep theological resources of Scripture, the Christian tradition, and the unique history of the congregation.
- Congregational worship should be integrated with the whole life of the congregation. It can serve as the "source and summit" from which all the practices of the Christian life flow. Worship both reflects and shapes the life of the church in education, pastoral care, community service, fellowship, justice, hospitality, and every other aspect of church life.
- The best worship practices feature not only good worship "content," such as discerning sermons, honest prayers, creative artistic contributions, celebrative and meaningful rituals for baptism and the Lord's Supper. They also arise of out of good process, involving meaningful contributions from participants, thoughtful leadership, honest evaluation, and healthy communication among leaders.

VITAL WORSHIP, HEALTHY CONGREGATIONS SERIES

The Vital Worship, Healthy Congregations Series is designed to reflect the kind of vibrant, creative energy and patient reflection that will promote worship that is both relevant and profound. It is designed to invite congregations to rediscover a common vision for worship, to sense how worship is related to all aspects of congregational life, and to imagine better ways of preparing both better "content" and "process" related to the worship life of their own congregations.

It is important to note that strengthening congregational life through worship renewal is a delicate and challenging task precisely because of the uniqueness of each congregation. This book series is not designed to represent a single denomination, Christian tradition, or type of congregation. Nor is it designed to serve as arbiter of theological disputes about worship. Books in the series will note the significance of theological claims about worship, but they may, in fact, represent quite different theological visions from each other, or from our work at the Calvin Institute of Christian Worship. That is, the series is designed to call attention to instructive examples of congregational life and to explore these examples in ways that allow readers in very different communities to compare and contrast these examples with their own practice. The models described in any given book may for some readers be instructive as examples to follow. For others, a given example may remind them of something they are already doing well, or something they will choose not to follow because of theological commitments or community history.

In the first volume in our series, *One Bread, One Body: Exploring Cultural Diversity in Worship,* Michael Hawn posed the poignant question "is there room for my neighbor at the table?" and explored what four multicultural congregations have to teach us about hospitality and the virtues of cross-cultural worship. His work helps us step back and reflect on the core identity of our congregations.

In this second volume, *Designing Worship Together: Models and Strategies for Worship Planning,* Howard Vanderwell and Norma deWaal Malefyt enter the trenches of weekly congregational life. They give us helpful insights into the process of how services are planned and led. It is hard to overstate the significance of this topic. For without a thoughtful, discerning, collaborative worship planning process, all manner of worship books, conferences, and renewal programs are likely either to make no inroads into the life of a given congregation or, when they do, to damage rather than renew congregational life.

By promoting encounters with instructive examples from various parts of the body of Christ, we pray that these volumes will help leaders make good judgments about worship in their congregations and that, by the power of God's Spirit, these congregations will flourish.

John D. Witvliet
Calvin Institute of Christian Worship

FOREWORD

I have known Norma deWaal Malefyt and Howard Vanderwell for at least half of the 25 years this book has been in the making. We have visited at conferences, talked intently about worship, and compared notes and experiences. The thoughtfulness with which they approached worship in those situations is reflected in this book. It also demonstrates the broad range of experience they bring to the problems we all encounter when we plan worship that arises from Scripture and reflects the indigenous style of the worshiping congregation.

While this book and the suggestions made for faithful and effective worship planning are extensive, the two issues that struck a chord in my mind and heart are the rootedness of their teaching in the biblical narrative and the strong connection their suggestions make with local churches.

First, I deeply appreciate their insistence that worship planning must arise from the biblical narrative. When worship is about God, the themes of worship will always be about God and God's mission to rescue creatures and creation. Worship that arises from the biblical narrative will express the language and vocabulary of the Christian tradition. Worship will emphasize God's holiness, mercy, justice, and love. Worship will also emphasize God's creativity—how God calls into being a creation marked with beauty and harmony. And worship will be attentive to the human condition, to the fall and the extension of the fall in our human culture making.

Worship also tells the story of God's involvement in history, God's efforts to show us the path to union with God. Worship focuses on how God has been at work through Abraham, Moses, Israel, and the prophets to point the way to God's incarnation in Jesus Christ; for it is in Jesus that God and humanity are united. In this union, Jesus does for us what we cannot do for ourselves. He is our voluntary sacrifice for sin. He defeats death and all that is evil. He rises to life. He brings us into union with God. He establishes the new creation now imaged in the church. The church, in its worship, remembers the saving deeds of God as it proclaims and enacts the story, and worship anticipates the culmination of history in the new heavens and the new earth, where all things are reconciled forever.

Norma and Howard understand this story and how its grammar and vocabulary constitute the very essence of Christian worship. They skill-fully help us plan our Sunday worship, services that follow the Christian year and all other worship gatherings, out of this narrative in which wor-ship is situated.

In a day when worship, born out of an antihistorical attitude, focuses on the self—what I need, what I want, what I do—it is refreshing to find a book that focuses on God yet is deeply concerned about the people en-gaged in worship. Howard and Norma's attention to the people who wor-ship is the second of many contributions that make this book especially helpful. While the content of God's narrative is applicable to all, Norma and Howard realize that the style in which God's saving deeds are pro-claimed will differ from community to community. The style in which God's narrative is remembered will differ from church to church, from place to place, from culture to culture. The story of God in the world can be told in a liturgical, traditional, contemporary, or blended way. The songs, the ritual acts, the preaching, the Eucharist, the prayers may reflect the style of street people, city dwellers, suburbanites, and rural farm folk. The style of worship may be indigenous to all cultures—Asian, African American, His-panic, Native American. No matter what worshipers' age, class, cultural situation, or geographical area, the principles set forth in this work are equally applicable.

I commend the work of Norma and Howard, because it is so rooted and yet so flexible. As you read these pages and encounter their wisdom drawn from biblical truth and personal experience, you will be led precept upon precept into a biblically sound and culturally attuned method to plan effective worship in your community.

Robert Webber
Myers Professor of Ministry
Director of Master of Arts in Worship and Spirituality
Northern Seminary

PREFACE

It has taken nearly 25 years to write this book. At least it's been in preparation for that long. What you find here has been developed in the laboratory of our own pastoral experience while serving as ministry staff, planning and leading worship.

We served on staff together for nearly 25 years, and they were strategic years, to say the least. During those years the Christian church experienced worship renewal, and often conflict over worship. We have experienced the exhilaration of leading worship week after week for a congregation that loves to worship well. We've experienced the deep satisfaction of planning worship services that lead people into the enriching presence of God. We've endured the satisfying pain of helping people worship in their most difficult times—sorrow, death, and national tragedy. We've felt overextended and overwhelmed at the unrelenting nature of the task—two different liturgies and sermons each week year-round. We've felt the pain of controversy and conflict over worship issues. We've felt the confusion of many conflicting expectations. We've been in circumstances where we faced theological and practical issues that sent us back to our study and research to sort out and clarify our own position on issues we never anticipated facing. The journey has been fascinating.

Our relationship began as that of a senior pastor and an organist of Hillcrest Christian Reformed Church of Hudsonville, Michigan, and developed into that of senior pastor and worship planner, and then to senior pastor and full-time director of music at Hillcrest. Like a pebble tossed into a pond, our work created ever-widening circles—from the two of us, to worship committee members, to a long list of volunteers listed in a worship resource bank, to a congregation that poured its heart into worship. We will forever be grateful to this congregation and the people with whom we were privileged to work. In particular, two individuals served as our most able and willing administrative assistants—Christy Brinks and Carol Somers, who provided not only technical help but also support and encouragement that helped us more than they often realized.

During our pastoral ministries we came to see the value of careful worship planning, but found that few tools and guidelines were available for our work. Many were writing about the theology of worship, the styles of worship, and the issues of music. Few were providing the practical nuts-and-bolts materials that worship planners need weekly. We had to develop our own as we went along, and providentially, our ministries spanned enough years that we could field-test them, revise them, and try again. Much of what you find here is the fruit of these years of ministry. We have not addressed issues of style. But you will find insights, guidelines, and tools that will aid worship planners regardless of what styles they choose. We aim also to provide materials that can be used in either a free or a liturgical tradition.

In chapter 1 we treat the subject of collaboration among ministry staff and worship planners. Those who collaborate well will find their work to be of higher quality and find their satisfaction increased. Those who cannot work well together will find great distress and disillusionment. In chapter 2 we examine the structure of supervisory and planning groups that will be helpful in the congregation, and we provide some models for consideration. Chapter 3 explores the strategic need for a "Congregational Worship Statement." Every group of worshipers includes a wide variety of expectations and perspectives on worship. A group must work through these and arrive at consensus about what worship is and how it will be enacted. Chapters 4 and 5 treat the practical aspects of planning. Constructing an annual worship calendar may seem a daunting task, but worship planning has better focus when those who do the planning think long-range first. And since the weekly worship planning sessions have far-reaching significance, we provide many ideas and tools for planners. Chapter 6 addresses the issue of worship evaluation, something everyone does—at least informally, if not formally—but that produces anxiety in all. We make a case for careful, deliberate, and constructive evaluation.

Though this material has been developed in the laboratory of our pastoral ministries, we are indebted to many others for their assistance and encouragement. We have already mentioned the Hillcrest congregation, which will always have a large place in our hearts. Our current ministries at the Calvin Institute of Christian Worship have continued to stir our love for worship. The director, Dr. John Witvliet, has been immensely helpful and encouraging. We are indebted to The Lilly Endowment, Inc., for its aid in our ministries and in making this project possible. The Alban Institute, whose ministry and publications have assisted us in our pastoral ministries, now enables us to reach out to others, and we give thanks for them. Our Alban editors, Beth Gaede and Jean Caffey Lyles, have been especially helpful, encouraging, understanding, and fun to work with! They have actually made the editing process both satisfying and enjoyable.

Many colleagues in ministry have been willing to partner with us and allow us to examine their experiences and draw on their observations. We've enjoyed our e-mail conversations with them about the subject of each chapter—Joel Boot, Doug Brouwer, Tim Carson, Karen DeMol, Paul Detterman, Fred Graham, Mary Hulst, Sue Imig, Stan Mast, Robert Mitman, Mark Nelesen, Greg Scheer, Carl Stam, Lisa Stracks, Annetta Vander Lugt, Mark Van't Hof, David Vroege, and Alan Whitmore. In addition, the students of PRTH 685—"Planning and Leading Congregational Worship," a course at Calvin Theological Seminary—provided helpful insight on many chapters.

A number of churches have made their worship statements public and available for consideration by others. We are grateful to Neland Avenue Christian Reformed Church and Church of the Servant in Grand Rapids, Michigan; First Presbyterian Church of Wheaton, Illinois; and Christ Lutheran Church of Sioux Falls, South Dakota. We owe a debt of gratitude to many other authors whose books and articles have encouraged and enlightened us. Many of them don't know us and we don't know them, but our ministries have been enriched by their efforts. It is our prayer that we may be able to do the same for others by this work.

We believe there is no greater Christian practice than that of worshiping God. While practical tools are important, even more important is the understanding that worship planning, like worship itself, must be done from a full heart. We couldn't wait for our Wednesday afternoon planning sessions. They became a sacred time in our ministries. And we found great joy and fulfillment in seeing all our efforts come together on Sunday as God's people came into his sacred presence. Our hope and prayer is that others may be encouraged in their ministries and find the same joy and fulfillment.

CHAPTER 1

THE CASE FOR COLLABORATION

Julia has been the worship coordinator at her church for three years. She has always had a deep love of worship and a desire to draw out the gifts of others for service in the church. She finds it fulfilling to worship in a well-planned service that uses the leadership gifts of several others from the congregation. It's important to her that all elements of a worship service fit together so that worshipers can better sense the focus and theme. But she has found it difficult to get information from her pastor early enough to allow for good planning. While Julia plans ahead, the pastor doesn't. During the past year or two he has gradually sensed the need to send her sermon information at least a couple of weeks in advance. Julia feels as though they are finally making progress in the planning process. But last week was a disaster. She had the pastor's sermon information, the Scripture passage, and even a couple of hymn suggestions a week and a half in advance. So Julia did her planning well, passed the information on to the others who were to be involved, and selected the hymns and service music accordingly. But on Saturday morning she discovered that the pastor had had a change of mind. The Scripture passage was changed, and so was the direction of the sermon. Consequently none of the liturgy and music worked well with the service of the Word. Julia was exasperated—and hurt!

Pastor Chris has always wanted to serve in a congregation where she could engage in team worship planning with a staff musician. She was certain that the ministry of the word and the ministry of music

*could be richly integrated in a parish where team planning was prac-
ticed. When she moved to a new pastorate, she was pleased to note
that the congregation had already employed a director of music. With
great eagerness she began a working relationship with Dean. But her
optimism was short-lived. Dean was so busy with competing commitments that he always seemed to be running behind schedule. Music was
not selected on time; choir members felt rushed in their preparation and
insecure when they sang in worship. Information for the bulletin was
often so sketchy that the secretaries found themselves either guessing
or making their own decisions about how the service should be ar-
ranged. A youth ensemble of instrumentalists was scheduled to ac-
company congregational singing, but Dean had not given them music
and instructions far enough in advance for them to prepare well. Even-
tually the relationship between Chris and Dean became strained, and
finally Chris lost heart. She also lost hope that she and the choir director could work out a satisfying method of team planning.*

*Carlos is a minister of music who likes to research hymnody to supple-
ment his congregation's song repertoire. A few months ago he found a
song that he thought would be an excellent sung prayer. He brought it
to Pastor Linda, who has very little musical talent. Linda loves to sing
and knows that song is a large part of a meaningful liturgy, but she
does not understand music and cannot read the notes. She had no
idea whether the song would be singable, but she liked the text and
encouraged Carlos to find ways to use it. Carlos worked with the song
and felt he could find good and fitting ways to include it in worship.
He involved others—an accompanist and an ensemble—to learn it
and prepared them to teach it to the congregation over a period of
time. The congregation now knows the song by heart, uses it often,
and finds it a valuable part of the liturgy. What started as a seed in
the study grew into a good experience for the whole congregation because several people with different gifts had worked together well.*

A generation or two ago most worship services were put together by one
person, usually the pastor. Either the congregation had a standard order of
service that required little or no creativity to prepare for, or the denomination published an official service book in which many of the standard ele-

ments of worship were provided. Others, particularly musicians, might participate in leading the service but certainly not in planning it. When the two of us began our ministries together in the late 1970s and early 1980s, worship planning consisted of selecting three songs to "plug in" to the standard order of service, phoning in the song numbers to the organist of the day—and worship planning was done!

That is no longer the case in many congregations. Solo worship planning is no longer the norm; it has given way to the team approach, both to enrich the planning process and to create healthy and broad ownership of worship leadership. Since no one person is able to provide creativity, variety, and freshness on a continuing basis, collaboration with others becomes necessary. Pastors who think they can go it alone will miss out on the valuable contributions that others can provide.

Collaboration is the word that best captures this experience of working together to craft worship liturgies. Collaborators are "co-laborers." They contribute from the field of their own gifts and passions. But they do not labor in isolation. Their labors are so interwoven that the final product is a composite. A group effort is genuinely the product of the entire group, not merely a modified solo plan.

F. Russell Mitman, a conference minister of the United Church of Christ and author of several books on worship leadership (*Worship in the Shape of Scripture* [Cleveland: Pilgrim Press, 2001], 95), speaks of collaboration as "orchestrating worship." Though some worship leaders might fear that orchestration involves manipulation for the sake of a certain effect, Mitman tries to recover the rightful and original meaning of "orchestrate." He says, "Orchestration involves putting everything together and creating a liturgical score that will enable the congregation to do their worship work" (103). Therefore, collaboration is the act of co-workers drawing resources together, arranging them in the liturgy, and preparing them well for the benefit of the congregation's worship. Just as a composer and a conductor help the various instruments in the orchestra work together harmoniously, so worship planners help all the worshipers to work together with one heart to worship God.

We have a model for such teaming in the work of the Holy Trinity as the Bible presents it to us. The Father, the Son, and the Holy Spirit exist and work in relationship with each other. Each has a role to play and unique tasks. Yet their workings, though often done individually, are a composite of all three. As a matter of fact, when the pastor pronounces the trinitarian benediction at the close of worship, a promise is made that all three persons of the Trinity will continue to co-labor on behalf of God's children throughout the week ahead. If the Trinity co-labors in this manner, we can expect that we as God's image-bearers are also called to work together.

We can see the same pattern in the worship of God's people in the Old Testament at both the tabernacle and the temple. Aaron may have been the first high priest, but a large number of Levites co-labored with him. The number of co-laborers needed was so large that God designated an entire tribe of Israel! Near the end of David's life he provided an accounting of the numbers of Levites, and we're told that there were 38,000 in all—24,000 to supervise the work of the temple, 6,000 as officers and judges, 4,000 as doorkeepers, and 4,000 musicians (1 Chron. 23:3-5). That situation must have involved a high level of collaboration! When Jerusalem was rebuilt and its worship reestablished under Ezra and Nehemiah after the exile, we find that both rebuilding the walls and leading worship were tasks widely distributed among the people. Nehemiah tells us about 74 Levites, 4,289 priests, and two choirs large enough to surround the city on the wall (Nehemiah 7 and 12). As the New Testament opens, we meet Zechariah, who was destined to be the father of John the Baptist. He was a priest from the division of Abijah. Lots were cast to determine which priests would go in before the Lord, and Zechariah was selected. When we catch a glimpse of a whole division of priests taking turns being on duty, and selections for the highest privilege being determined by lot, we know that a great deal of co-laboring took place.

But perhaps the clearest pattern for collaboration is in the New Testament teaching on spiritual gifts. The picture Paul paints of the church is not of a body in which one person has all the gifts and sets all the plans. It is rather a body whose members are all gifted. None are left without gifts; no one possesses all the available gifts. Paul says, "Now to each one the manifestation of the Spirit is given for the common good" (1 Cor. 12:7). Then after listing a variety of possible spiritual gifts, he adds, "All these are the work of one and the same Spirit, and he gives them to each one, just as he determines" (1 Cor. 12:11). Paul sees the church, even the church at Corinth about which he has shed so many tears, as a body of believers who have all been granted gifts by the Holy Spirit so that they can participate in the work of the church in the world.

Marva Dawn, noted Lutheran theologian and author, coins a word to express this New Testament teaching. She says, "The faithful Church has never been—and should never be—a democracy nor a hierarchy. Rather, it is a *Spiritocracy,* a Body governed by the Spirit's empowering with Christ as the Head, and a *charismacracy,* a word I coined to signify leadership by means of Spirit-endowed gifts (*charisma* in Greek)" (Dawn, *How Shall We Worship?* [Wheaton, Ill: Tyndale House, 2003], 147). The charismacracy that plans worship, she explains, includes the gifts of the pastor, church musicians of many sorts, and planning groups, which include a diversity of people.

A GREATER GOOD FOR WORSHIP PLANNERS

Collaboration will not only honor God's method of distributing a variety of spiritual gifts among us, but it will also provide many practical benefits. When church leaders co-labor they will find their service richer, more satisfying, and less frustrating.

1. *Planners will experience vastly increased creativity.* One person planning alone may possess some creativity, but it will soon run dry unless it is stimulated by an exchange of ideas and evaluations with others. Planning discussions within a team can stir up creative ideas that no one would have thought of alone. We have always found in worship co-laboring that one plus one equals not two but four because of such stimulated creativity.

2. *Planners will benefit from a wide range of insight, knowledge, and skills.* When a group gets together to plan worship, all participants bring their own insights and experiences and contribute to the whole. The musicians know the songs and repertoire that would best suit the focus of a particular service. The youth coordinator knows the teenagers best and understands how they can participate. Sunday school teachers will know what songs the children know. Others will understand the pain and the joy in the congregation from their personal relationships within the community of faith. Still others can suggest where visuals and drama may make their contributions. Planning together can spark ideas none of the planners would have come up with alone.

How Collaboration Benefits Worship Planners

1. Vastly increased creativity
2. A wider ranger of insight, knowledge, and skills
3. Greater ownership of what has been planned
4. A healthy corrective
5. A healthy variety in worship

---

3. *Planners experience greater ownership of what they have planned.* When a group gets together to plan for Advent or Lent, you can be sure that they will come to worship during that season with a greater sense of investment in those services than they would experience otherwise. We own what we invest in, and we take a greater interest in what we "own."

4. *Multiple planners provide a healthy corrective.* One person alone can easily be myopic. We think we are seeing clearly, yet we may have lost our objectivity. We have our own ideas and preferences, but we fail to realize that some others do not share them. We revert to our own favorite themes without realizing that we have overemphasized them. We make suggestions that seem good at the outset, but that on closer examination would not be wise. Yet none of us can be truly objective about ourselves and our own ideas. We need others to talk with us, raise questions, add insights, and engage in careful evaluations. A group that can trust and be honest with each other will avoid many dangerous pitfalls.

5. *Multiple planners can promote a healthy variety in worship.* A few generations ago people welcomed worship marked by "sameness." The same voice in the same tone using the same phrases, and weekly worship in the same pattern, were welcome. Not today! Even the more liturgical churches are seeking variations that are more ecumenical and global, and that involve various styles. Communication in our society has broadened our understanding of the church in a way that increases our desire for richer and more diverse worship experiences. Our culture thrives on variety. In addition, our personal experiences during the week have been so varied that we each come with different needs and expectations. Multiple worship planners can provide such variety better than a lone planner. But they can also supervise the pace and quality of the variations.

GOOD FOR CHURCHES

Not only will worship planners find their tasks richer and more satisfying, but congregations served by collaborative planning teams will find that the worship life of their church has a different tone.

1. *Congregations will be enriched when they appreciate the heritage of others.* It is important for each of us to appreciate our own heritage. But it's also important that we learn to appreciate the heritage of fellow Christians. Nearly every Christian congregation has a less homogeneous heritage today than it had a generation ago, and it has become customary to draw elements into the worship service from other traditions. We learn through such patterns, methods, readings, songs, prayers, and sacramental actions to live into the worship life of other Christians and appreciate both our heritage and theirs. Worship planners can represent a variety of heritages or can jointly study heritages other than their own.

2. *Churches will worship with greater balance.* When worship is planned with little collaborative creativity, it has less freedom and can more easily become locked into the same pattern and structure. We must ask ourselves whether those who enter our worship services now, and those who will look back on them 25 years from now, will find that we satisfactorily balanced structure and spontaneity, freshness and continuity, lay and clerical leadership, local focus and global awareness.

3. *Each worship service has a consistent theme.* When different people are responsible for separate parts of the worship service and fail to collaborate, strange things can happen. Planners who do not plan together can easily go in different directions, and a worshiper caught in a worship service with elements that move in multiple and sometimes opposite directions will experience dissonance and confusion. We're thinking of a recent worship service: the guest pastor was preaching on the virtues of the Christian life from Colossians 3, but the guest musicians had brought only songs that focused on the second coming of Christ. The service had no consistent theme throughout because planners did not work together.

4. *A worship theme can be reinforced in multiple ways.* Not all worshipers have the same needs. Not all are of the same age. A worship service

How Collaboration Benefits the Church

1. Our own heritage will be enriched by appreciating the heritage of others.
2. We worship with greater balance.
3. Worship services have a consistent theme.
4. A worship theme can be reinforced in multiple ways.
5. Worship services will involve greater integration.

that presents its theme in only one way may therefore be beneficial for some but not for others. If multiple planners are involved in presenting the central theme in a variety of ways, the result can be of greater benefit to a larger number of people. What the preached word may fail to do, the ministry of music may do, and vice versa, or a responsive litany may reinforce the points given in a message.

5. *Worship services will involve greater integration.* In earlier years the worship services of some traditions had two parts—preliminaries and preaching. In highly liturgical traditions, the focus of the entire liturgy involved movement toward the Table. In a charismatic tradition the parts are often praise and teaching. In all three instances, the two sections may be unrelated to each other. How much richer is worship when a constant theme is carried forward by all parts of the service—the preaching, the songs, the anthems, the readings, the visuals, the prayers, and the sacraments. One constant theme expressed by all integrated efforts brings us back to the orchestration idea again! Each element stands on its own as a unique dimension of worship but gains strength when it is carefully integrated with the other worship elements.

IT WON'T BE EASY

The case for collaboration is a strong one. The pattern God sets before us in the Bible certainly encourages it. The benefits for both the congregation and those who must plan and lead worship are convincing.

However, we must be realistic and admit that choosing the path of collaboration entails some obstacles, sometimes looming so large that they have led some to give up, lose heart, or avoid trying to plan collaboratively. We've been somewhat surprised in consulting on this matter with colleagues at conferences or through correspondence to learn how quick they are to list the obstacles. It's easy to put together a long list. We'll set most of the common obstacles before you, not to suggest that you'll face all these, but to recognize that you could potentially discover these roadblocks on your journey. Rare is the church that runs up against only one obstacle.

1. *Incompatible views of worship.* We place this obstacle at the top of the list as the most common and nettlesome barrier that most of us face. No one needs to be reminded that many differing views of worship are found within the Christian church today. No one needs to be reminded that people hold these views with great fervor and passion. In some traditions people are appointed or volunteer to serve on a worship planning team. Think what happens when the team members have incompatible views of worship. That incompatibility becomes a serious issue when each member is convinced that he or she represents sizable elements within the congregation. The whole phenomenon of a "worship war" or the fear of a worship war could dominate the worship planning arena. To function well, the planning group must avoid this scenario. The leadership of the church must work hard to establish a clear vision of worship for the congregation, must articulate it well, and must communicate it to the membership. This work must also include educational efforts, so that the congregation as a whole will own the vision. Accomplishing this task requires that the leaders make a careful study of the biblical and theological principles of worship, as well as of the culture and the needs of the congregation. Once articulated and communicated to the congregation, this vision gives the planning group the basis on which to do its work. While the planning group must not fall into the trap of tunnel vision and must remain open to new ideas and broad-ranging discussions, the members of the planning group must own a common vision of worship.

2. *Insufficient time is available.* The people who could work well collaboratively are usually people with multiple commitments. Trying to find a convenient evening for a group to meet on a regular basis can be difficult. The larger the group, the larger the obstacle. At every meeting a member or two may be missing and lose the continuity of the work. Other members may show up late because

they have other commitments. The pastor also experiences a tight schedule. The calendar is full, and finding time for another meeting is a challenge. Sitting in a slow-moving meeting will tempt even the most motivated pastor to think the work could be done more efficiently if it were done "solo." The group will need to negotiate together, establish a regular meeting time to which all will commit, and encourage one another to make worship planning a priority. One whose schedule cannot be accommodated may choose to drop out of the group rather than alter his or her priorities.

3. *A failure of partnerships.* Collaboration does not allow for people to work independently with their own preferences. Collaboration calls for partnerships in which people merge their ideas, their passions, their efforts, and their concerns. A planning group must be a team, and teams require partnerships in which the participants trust and respect each other and are willing to join one another's efforts. However, the saboteurs of such partnerships are many. Imagine a group in which one person seems to delight in resisting the leadership of another, or one in which two of the members have a personality clash that makes it impossible for them to function smoothly together. Beware of groups in which members are jealous of the attention or credit someone else gets. Someone has wisely said, "There's no limit to what can be accomplished if you don't care who gets the credit." The success of such groups will be greatly diminished, and working within those groups will not be a pleasant experience until some of the wrinkles are ironed out. Working together closely within a group requires a certain mind-set and skill-set, and the members of such a team should be selected with these criteria in mind.

4. *Some don't carry their weight.* A planning team is usually made up of volunteers, and some volunteers will be less motivated than others. If all the volunteers are eager and willing to carry out their responsibilities, they will not only contribute well to the work themselves but will provide inspiration and motivation to others. However, if some fail to complete assignments, or come to meetings unprepared, not only does the work suffer; in addition, others' motivation can be seriously dampened. A negative cycle is set in motion, endangering the effectiveness of the group. People who do

not carry their weight need to be encouraged to higher levels of motivation, or, if the matter cannot be resolved or if their behavior stems from understandable causes, they should perhaps be encouraged to find another avenue of service.

5. *Political poll taking.* In North American culture every organization, including the Christian church, is marked by a wide diversity of opinions and preferences. And in the area of worship, opinions and preferences are held with seemingly unequaled passion. If the church is a totally democratic organization, then polls are crucial, and popular opinion and majority vote decide the issues of the day. However, the church abides by truth given to us by God—in direct commands, in principles to be applied, and in models to be emulated. The church approaches every issue not by taking a poll, but by contemplating Scripture. We don't begin with our own preferences and hope later to find Scripture passages to support them. We begin from a posture of expectant learning and receiving, gleaning from Scripture ways in which our own preferences might be challenged. Worship leaders of all kinds must serve as models of that posture of learning rather than reinforcing a pattern of political poll taking. Yet some don't. They come to their leadership role believing that they are to function as "ecclesiastical politicians" who must return periodically to their district to see what the voters want. These members will come to a planning meeting with reports on what they have heard and what "the people like" (usually gleaned from a very selective sampling). Or they will suggest that before major decisions are made, a survey should be taken to determine "the mind of the people." Such polling causes a planning session to deteriorate into devising ways to satisfy the largest number of people most of the time. Vision is lost. Passion is dissipated. And the group soon feels that its planning is held hostage to popular opinion.

6. *A competitive spirit.* Competition is usually considered a virtue in team play in our sports-oriented society. Players with a healthy spirit of competition practice longer, play harder, and go farther. But a competitive spirit is of no benefit to a planning team within the church. The members of this team set their competitive spirits aside when they join the collaborative effort. Those who prefer the contemporary may not compete with those who prefer the more

---

Obstacles to Collaboration

1. Incompatible views of worship
2. Insufficient available time
3. Failure of partnerships
4. Unwillingness of some to carry their weight
5. Political poll taking
6. A competitive spirit
7. Tunnel vision
8. Personal agendas
9. Differences between pastor and musician
10. Failure of the pastor to plan ahead

---

traditional, and vice versa. Organists and pianists may not compete with each other for leadership roles. The pastor and the musician may not compete. Directors of the children's choirs and the adult choirs may not compete for more prominent roles for their groups within the service. The music, drama, or dance ministries may not compete for attention. The common goal—to lead rich and vital worship for the glory of God and the benefit of the church—must always be in the forefront. The planning team cannot afford to waste its time and energy on internal competition.

7. *Tunnel vision.* People with tunnel vision go through life with blinders on and can see things only in a narrow focus. They are not able to see the landscape around them. They are not able to listen carefully to other people's insights and ideas. They fail to understand that other, related issues must be discussed and evaluated. They see things one way, and usually that way is shaped by their past experiences or by the preferences of a certain power group to which they are currently listening. You will hear them say, "If it was good enough for our parents and grandparents, then it should be good enough for us!" or "If you go in that direction, we're in for trouble. Those folks just won't like this, and you'll hear from them!" or "The only way to liven up our worship is to get a better amplifying system and a good praise team." People with tunnel vision usually display a great deal of tenacity. Tunnel vision often disqualifies a person from serving productively on a planning team.

8. *Personal agendas.* A related obstacle is the matter of personal agendas. Every meeting should have an agenda planned, printed, and given

to each member before the meeting. The goal for every planning session should be vital worship for the church. That is *the* agenda! The secondary agenda of each member of the group is using his or her insights, gifts, and experiences to further the larger agenda of vital worship. But often people bring personal agendas that may run counter to the larger agenda. We've experienced members coming to a committee or planning group determined to push one cause. When team members harbor such an intent, they become potential saboteurs to the work of the group. Only when all are willing to set aside personal agendas and submit their personal preferences to those of the group will they serve the cause of the main agenda.

9. *Differences between pastor and musician.* Since these two are often the key people on a worship planning team, their relationship and compatibility, or lack of it, will greatly influence the effectiveness of the planning process. Thomas Troeger and Carol Doran, a pastor-musician team who have written about revitalizing congregational worship, remind us that "the division that exists between music and theology, especially in the training of people for these different callings, is often acted out in the relationship between musician and pastor" (Troeger and Doran, *Trouble at the Table* [Nashville: Abingdon, 1992], 78). Great care must be given to forming a healthy relationship. If the relationship is collegial and trusting, much good will result. If they do not trust each other and are not willing to listen to and learn from each other, they will not be able to work together well, and the work of the planning group of which they are a part will be significantly more difficult. The risk that these two people will have differences is high, for a variety of reasons. They often have different training, one in theology and the other in choral conducting or organ performance. Seminaries teach too little about music, and musicians often learn too little theology. The temperament of one may be quite different from the other. Each may be concerned with turf protection. It's easy for conflict and suspicion to arise between them. However, what a difference it will make in the planning group, in the worship life of the church, and in the church as a whole, if these two can serve collaboratively, with both making their own unique contributions while greatly

appreciating each other's contribution. Later in this chapter we say more about what it takes to be an able collaborator, but for now suffice it to say that the church where pastor and musician are a compatible team is richly blessed.

10. *The failure of the pastor to plan.* The key person in the entire planning process is the pastor. The Scripture and the sermon shape the focus of a worship service, not the other way around. Since the pastor is the one who selects the Scripture and prepares the sermon, the pastor becomes the key person in the planning process. Even when churches follow the lectionary, pastors will still make decisions about which of the passages they will select for the sermon and how it will be focused. A pastor's selections will be the primary determinant in shaping the focus of a worship service. It can't be any other way. All other planners need to know what the pastor will be preaching about before the rest of the planning process can get under way. Those who will provide the visuals must know what images (or major sermon points) to project on the screen, and what banners and paraments to use. Those who select the anthems must know what themes will be appropriate. Those who plan the readings in evangelical traditions must know the content they are expected to have. Congregational music selections must be based on the focus of the service. All of this work will require time—weeks and sometimes months. The pastor who provides selections comfortably far ahead of time will serve other planners well and provide a healthy planning process. The pastor who does not and will not plan ahead will hold everybody up, and greatly frustrate the team members and the process of planning.

Healthy collaboration requires trusting people who respect one another, listen to one another, express their thoughts openly, and continue to grow together. A collaborative team is, in short, a microcosm of what the body of Christ is called to be. But primarily, developing healthy co-laboring takes time. The collaborative planning process cannot be rushed, so time may be one of the biggest gifts that we give each other.

The late Erik Routley, a noted author, composer, and expert on music in the church, pointedly expressed the urgency of compatible relationships, saying:

It will remain bad theology so long as [the] theologian and the artist refuse to communicate with one another; as long as the theologian regards the artist as fundamentally a temperamental trifler, and the artist the theologian as an obstinate and ignorant theorist, the best we shall get is patronage from church to music, together with tentative moralisms from musicians to musicians. At worst it will be, as it often in practice is, a wicked waste of an opportunity for glorifying God through fruitful partnership [Routley, *Church Music and Theology* (Philadelphia: Muhlenberg Press, 1959), 110].

While the list of obstacles might seem daunting and discouraging, we raise these considerations so that you might be realistic at the outset. If you are realistic about obstacles like these, you will be better able to overcome them. And, more important, such realism will lead us to pray for God's grace, strength, and wisdom to handle such obstacles. If there is any place in the church where grace must win out, it should be in the collaborative efforts of worship planners. At a recent meeting of worship planning teams, one pastor reported that a non-negotiable in all his group's planning is that grace pervades the process.

That's why we move now to think about the kinds of people who will be able to work together.

QUALIFICATIONS OF WORSHIP PLANNERS

If such great benefits are experienced when planners collaborate well, and if such significant obstacles must be overcome, then we want to choose carefully who will participate in the planning process. (In chapter 2 we address such matters as the organization of planning groups and whether members ought to be volunteers or appointees.) The church that places people on such teams to "get them involved" or to satisfy various elements of the congregation is asking for trouble. A worship planning team is so critical a part of the life of any congregation that those who serve in this group ought to have the clearest qualifications of any group in church. Worship planners should manifest qualifications of the heart, the head, and the hand.

Qualifications of the Heart

Worship is a spiritual encounter with God. Almost anyone can plan a patriotic rally or a company picnic, but only spiritually healthy people can expect to be effective in planning worship. Collaborators need, therefore, the qualifications of the heart listed below.

1. *A sense of the holiness of God.* The Bible teaches that worshipers are coming into the presence of a God who is holy, infinite, and majestic. Particularly in the early chapters of Revelation, we learn that the God we worship is enthroned and worthy of praise. Worshipers must therefore be eager to give God honor and glory. The exclamation of the angels and the church should always be ringing in the hearts of worship planners: "Amen! Praise and glory and wisdom and thanks and honor and power and strength be to our God for ever and ever. Amen!" (Rev. 7:12).

2. *A sense of priestlike leadership.* Though it is true that Jesus Christ is the only mediator between God and humans, worship leaders stand in that very holy and special place as representatives of Christ between God and his people. At times they will speak for God to the people; at other times for the people to God. At times this dual role can seem very frightening. Who are we to write words that people will speak? Who are we to determine what types of songs they will sing, or the spirit in which they will sing them? Who are we to determine which prayers, and for which needs, they will pray? And who are we to orchestrate this encounter that we hope will create the holiest hour in the week? Yes, frightening at times! But also an overwhelming privilege! What can be more beautiful than aiding the children of God in praying well, in crying to God, in giving testimony to their faith, and in expressing their praise? Yes, the worship planner stands in between, and anyone who aims to stand there should have a deep sense of awe, privilege, and even fright.

3. *A growing spiritual life.* Not only should worship planners be committed Christians, they should also evidence the passion of a healthy spiritual life. They must faithfully practice the disciplines of the Christian life—repenting and confessing, reading and meditating on the Scriptures, and engaging in personal prayer. In other words, they should be people in whom the work and the influence of the Holy Spirit are obvious—not that they have successfully overcome all questions and struggles, but that they are seeking to grow in the faith. Healthily growing Christians are the ones who can most sensitively plan worship for others.

Qualifications of the Heart

1. A sense of the holiness of God
2. A sense of priestlike leadership
3. A growing spiritual life
4. A love for the church
5. Pastoral sensitivity

4. *Love for the church.* Those of us who love the Lord must love the church, which he called his body. Our love must be not only for the universal worldwide body that we cannot see but also for this tangible and visible part that is before us, with its strengths and weaknesses, beauty and warts, successes and failures. We must be deeply and compassionately in love with the congregation to which we belong and for which we are planning worship. How can we plan worship for a church that we do not love? And loving involves knowing and understanding the history, the story, the culture, and the personality of our congregation. We'll be motivated to invest our spirit heartily into planning when it's for a church we love. When we plan something others don't like or something that does not achieve the goal we had in mind, it will be easier for others to be gracious when they know it comes from one who genuinely loves the church.

5. *Pastoral sensitivity.* Yes, a pastor must be sensitive to the needs and hurts of parishioners. Worship planners should have the same quality. Let them be warm people who know others, love others, celebrate their joys, feel their pain, and care deeply. Pastors who stand before the congregation on Sunday and can look out over them with a deeply caring heart will see the pain and struggle from one pew to another. They will see a family that bears turmoil that nobody else knows about. They will remember the health concerns in some homes. They will remember the searing doubts one parishioner has expressed and the depression that another has dealt with. And when pastors lead in worship—when they speak, pray, and give a blessing—they will remember all those needs, and they will compassionately address them. The worshipers will sense an empathy coming through. Other planners must manifest the same empathy. The musician with such a pastoral sensitivity will be a different kind of musician, and you'll know it in the music played. You'll sense it in the way the congregational singing is led. And when

worship planners have that pastoral sensitivity, the liturgy they create will have "soul." It's that sixth sense of "knowing" what worship should be.

Qualifications of the Head

Serving as a worship planner is a significant task because such people are able to influence and help shape the life of a congregation. Such a person ought to possess intellectual qualifications that will ensure wise leadership. There are half a dozen marks of such qualification.

1. *A theology of worship.* Since each congregation has a wide range of opinions and preferences about worship, those who plan worship should be knowledgeable about the biblical principles of worship. Let them be people who study and grow, who take an interest in the issues of worship, and are continually clarifying their understanding of the issues involved. If they are to avoid being swayed by every new wind in worship trends, they must be anchored well. They should know, understand, support, and ably defend the statement of worship of their congregation. That doesn't mean that membership on the team should be limited to those who have received formal education in theology, but team members should be people who are well read and informed, regardless of their level of formal education. Let them be people who love to learn and keep on doing so.

2. *The primacy of worship.* One of the holiest hours in the life of any congregation is the time of worship. The worship hour is not one slice of the congregational pie among others. It is the prime time of that congregation's life. It is the time when the whole family gathers. The worship life of the church shapes the entire church spiritually. Anyone who participates in the planning of worship must be certain of that and be inspired by the task of shaping that holy hour. Kennon Callahan, church consultant and best-selling author (*Dynamic Worship* [San Francisco: HarperCollins, 1994], 83), says that such people ought to be "first day of the week people." It was on the first day of the week that Christ arose, and the church discovered the amazing reality of his resurrection. Ever since, the church has lived

with the conviction that worship is the entrance to the week and that it launches God's people along the time line set for them. Those who work together at planning first-day worship should be people committed to the primacy of worship in the life of the church.

3. *Submission for the sake of the whole.* We have spoken previously about how easily planning can be sabotaged by team members who seek their own agenda instead of the good of the whole group. Any member who joins the planning team should therefore make a conscious decision to submit their own wishes to the desires of the group. Only a certain kind of person can do this—one who has been captured by Jesus Christ, one who is deeply committed to both Christ and his body, and one who is secure. Only someone who can set aside personal desires is qualified to serve on such a team.

4. *Compatible relationships.* Compatibility can be hard to measure, but its importance cannot be overemphasized. All team members must be compatible with one another on several levels—in their commitment:

- to Jesus Christ as their Savior and Lord,
- to the life of the church,
- to the faith confessed by the church,
- to the worship of the church, and
- to the specific vision of worship in their congregation.

But compatibility must also exist on a personal level. Members of a group need not always see eye-to-eye with one another. As a matter of fact, if they do, they are probably not being totally honest. However, they ought to trust and respect one another. A planning team ought to be able to be open, candid, and loving with one another—and at times confrontational. This trust and respect will not develop without a firm intention to work together. For instance, the pair who serve as the pastor/musician team at St. Matthew's Church of Perkasie, Pennsylvania, describe themselves as "kindred spirits" because of their shared love for the congregation and their ability to think and plan together. Their "kindred spirit" relationship makes it possible for them to plan weekly and to spend a couple of days each quarter at a local library charting out long-range worship

Qualifications of the Head

1. A theology of worship
2. The primacy of worship
3. Individual's submission for the sake of the whole
4. Compatible relationships
5. An understanding of the planner's role
6. Ability to communicate
7. Knowledge of the congregation

plans. They obviously have made a conscious decision to work together compatibly.

5. *Understanding the role of a planner.* Worship planning is a unique task. What a privilege to design an event that will enable people to meet God and to create a setting in which worshipers of all ages can experience awe, wonder, and mystery! Anyone who doesn't approach that task with a sense of inadequacy doesn't understand it very well. The planner should understand that this craft needs to be carefully learned and developed. In planning we are to be faithful to the truth of God, to the experiences and needs of the worshipers, and to the heritage of a congregation. A planner ought to respect and seek out the gifts of all others who are able and willing to be involved in contributing to worship leadership. A planner should create an environment in which they are able to serve well. But planners must also understand the matter of accountability—not to popular opinion and preferences—but to God and to the worship vision of the congregation.

6. *Ability to communicate.* Words are the tools of all worship planning. Many of those words are printed in an order of worship, woven into prayers and readings, combined to form a sermon, or set to music so that we can sing our faith and cry out our needs. But many of the words a planning team employs are private and will be expressed in group discussions within its meetings. A participant ought to be able to find words to express ideas and convey thoughts accurately. A participant with limited verbal skills will make little contribution, or create uncertainty and confusion in the planning team, yet most certainly could use his or her gifts in other supportive roles—visual arts or music among others.

7. *Knowledge of the congregation.* Every Christian congregation has its own personality and culture. Events, people, and issues have shaped it in a unique way. Its culture and personality will also have a profound effect on the way the congregants worship the Lord. To ignore such a fact, or to be ignorant of it, will lead to some significant missteps by worship planners. Those who plan worship for a given congregation should know its history, know the issues and events that have shaped it, and should understand its unique personality. This doesn't mean that only long-term members can serve best (for maybe they are too close to be objective) but that those who serve in leadership roles must make the effort to listen to others and to enter the story and history of the congregation.

Qualifications of the Hand

The heart and the head may be healthy, but worship planners must be available. The readiness to put oneself forward for service we call "the qualification of the hand." It involves:

1. *A willingness to volunteer.* People who volunteer are offering a valuable gift to the church. However, most studies show that many people will serve *only when personally asked to serve.* The face-to-face or telephoned request overcomes their reticence to volunteer. We have tried to make it easier for folk to volunteer by providing a "Worship Resource Bank Survey" at the beginning of each liturgical season. We've made a sample copy available on page 30 of this chapter that you are welcome to use. During an offering the congregants are given a list of all the roles of service in the worship life of the congregation and are encouraged to indicate the ones for which they will be available. We have found that with the use of this form, the number of volunteers has steadily increased year by year. We have also learned to take seriously all offers to serve and to use all who volunteer. To that end, we've kept a record of each person's involvement.

2. *A willingness to schedule the necessary time.* We must back up our offers to serve by clearing time in our calendars. Worship planning takes time. Attendance at regular meetings is necessary. Assignments must be faithfully carried out. People who say they will serve, but

Qualification of the Hand

1. A willingness to volunteer
2. A willingness to schedule the necessary time
3. The fulfillment of all assigned tasks
4. Practice and growth in God's gifts

fail to make time available, are sending contradictory messages that discourage others. But the person who makes time to attend meetings and complete tasks faithfully is a valuable contributor to the life of the group.

3. *The fulfillment of all assigned tasks.* The work of worship planning cannot all be done in a group meeting. Group discussions will involve planning worship schedules, clarifying themes, brainstorming ideas, and selecting participants. But many specific tasks will be completed by team members outside the meeting. The spirit of the group is damaged by a member who consistently fails to complete assigned tasks, just as its spirit is greatly encouraged by those who can be counted on regularly to complete all assignments. We, like you, have been in groups where certain members could be counted on to show up at the meeting with unfinished work and to make rather transparent excuses for failing to complete the assignment.

4. *Practice and growth in God's gifts.* Worship planning, while not requiring that only the perfect participate, encourages us to commit ourselves to offer our best to God in worship. Therefore, whatever our gift may be, we must evidence a commitment to use it well, to continue our growth, and to practice it regularly. A musician knows that playing the organ, the piano, or any other musical instrument requires focused practice time. Other roles do too. Structuring litanies, shaping meaningful prayers, reading Scripture, writing dramas, designing a liturgical dance, creating visuals, and participating in choral rehearsals must all receive faithful and energetic effort so that what we offer to God is our best.

Rich is that church in which people qualified in heart, head, and hand step forward and serve together for the sake of vital and enriching worship! The congregation will be healthier, the team members will find their work satisfying, and God will be honored. Since it is essential to reach a good understanding with team members, we have included a sample letter on page 32 of this chapter that can be sent to those newly chosen for a planning team.

THE INTEGRATION OF ROLES

Until now we have not said much about how all the various roles in worship planning can be integrated. Planning team members must not function like independent golfers, who play their own rounds, but like a basketball team whose members make no move without considering the others.

A healthy integration of all roles begins with the agreement by all that worship is "the work of the people"—that is what the word "liturgy" means. Worship in the assembly of the congregation is corporate. No one person does the work; it is rather the work of all the people. Those who plan and lead have a strategic role behind the scenes in preparing the worship service. But when the worship begins, a rhythm must prevail in the dialogue of God's voice to us and our voice to him. A rhythm should also distinguish the alternation of moments when the worship leader speaks for God and moments when he or she speaks for the people. It is true that worship requires leaders in many roles. The two key roles will be that of the pastor and that of the church musician. The number and variety of other roles will be determined by the practices and traditions of each congregation, but regardless of how many there are, integration is important.

The pastor will have the lead role. By virtue of training, knowledge of the congregation, responsibility for preaching, and what congregations expect of clergy leaders, the pastor will and should contribute the most to the overall worship direction and theme. We have previously pointed to the pastor's responsibility to plan ahead, so that other planners will have time to make their preparations. But good pastors will not attempt to dominate the planning process. They will know when to be prominent and when to fade into the background and allow others to lead.

The church musician will also have a key role, because the full integration in worship of music ministries will depend on his or her involvement in the full process. This person will be the chief musician of the congregation and may be a director or minister of music, a coordinator or administrator, or even the organist, but whatever the title, he or she is responsible for all aspects of the music life of the congregation. Though the pastor will take the lead in shaping the theme and direction of worship, the church musician must take the lead in shaping the song of congregational worship.

A partnership between these two is absolutely essential. When they can work together compatibly and trustingly, their healthy partnership will serve the church well. When they refuse or are unable to work well together, the result is great damage to the worship life of the church.

Paul Westermeyer, professor of church music at Luther Seminary in St. Paul, Minnesota (and cantor and director of the Master of Sacred Music program at St. Olaf College, Northfield, Minnesota), points out some of the causes of particularly damaging nonpartnerships, identifying a dozen examples (*The Church Musician* [Minneapolis: Augsburg Fortress, 1997], 87-94). Notice how either the pastor or the musician can be the instigator of the difficulty. In churches where more people are included in the planning, any of them could become the instigator. Westermeyer identifies these:

1. The pastor is a manipulator.
2. The pastor is a dictator.
3. The pastor controls by chaos.
4. The pastor assumes the musician is a trifler.
5. The pastor assumes the musician is a hired hand.
6. The musician assumes a business relationship with the pastor.
7. The musician assumes the pastor is a theorist.
8. The musician functions as a technician.
9. The musician is a dictator.
10. The musician is a manipulator.
11. The pastor and musician have no dialogue.
12. The pastor and musician have no dialogue with malice.

In addition to these two leaders, we believe that others will also serve in key roles. Each congregation will have to select the model of the working relationships it chooses to follow. We address the matter of various models in chapter 2. However, here are the most common ones. Some of these will be identified with a single person; others will be groups of people working as a team.

1. *The Pastor.* The key person who sets the direction for worship by the selections made for preaching.

2. *The Church Musician.* The second key person who complements the work of the pastor by setting a consistent and compatible direction for all the music ministries of the church.
3. *The Music Staff.* Other key people who are either instrumentalists, directors of ensembles and choral groups, or people who participate in them.
4. *Worship Assistants.* Those who lead in the worship service by reading Scripture, leading litanies, and offering prayers.
5. *Artistic Staff.* Those responsible for drama, dance, and all visual preparations within the worship space, such as hangings, banners, flower arrangements, and liturgical symbols.
6. *Support Roles.* Those who prepare the worship space—ushers, acolytes, sound and video technicians, and others.

Some but not all of these people will be represented on the worship planning team. Yet all must be informed regularly of the plans for the worship seasons and the needs for each particular worship service. All must understand how their task fits into the total picture of worship planning.

Each of these people must use accurate images to think clearly of their role. John Witvliet, director of the Calvin Institute of Christian Worship, points to five images or roles by which worship leaders perceive themselves (Witvliet, *Worship Seeking Understanding* [Grand Rapids: Baker Academic, 2003], 280). Those five are:

1. *Pastoral Planners.* These planners love people, understand their desires and needs, and aim graciously to lead them into the presence of God for an encounter that will enrich them and bring honor to God.
2. *Craftspeople.* These planners craft words into meaningful messages and readings, make music, and prepare visuals.
3. *Directors and Coordinators.* These planners recruit people, assign their tasks, coach them, conduct rehearsals, and finalize all arrangements.
4. *Performers.* These planners preach sermons, play the organ, sing, and participate in a drama or dance for the benefit of others.
5. *Spiritual Engineers.* These planners somehow see themselves as responsible for inspiring people, creating moments that are packed with spiritual power, and "managing the encounter with God."

Witvliet says he has spoken with many worship leaders in a number of denominations, and, when asked how they regard their role, they have usually offered descriptions that fall into one of the last four categories (2 through 5). However, he is certain that the best image for all participants to work with is the pastoral image. Planning and leading worship is essentially a pastoral task. The pastoral task of all those involved in worship planning is the one thread that must run through all roles. It serves as the only consideration that will fully and healthily integrate all roles.

THE CARE OF THE TEAM

In speaking about those who collaborate on a worship planning team, we have not touched on one basic, though often overlooked, fact. All team members are human beings. To say that is to add a whole new element to our considerations. People experience joy and sadness, delight and frustration. They can be excited or discouraged. They can be both secure and fragile. They all have needs, and they will seek to have those needs met. Therefore, it is not only essential to place people in the appropriate roles and integrate all roles well; it is also vital to care for them well as they serve in those roles. The care of volunteers is an important and often neglected aspect of the work of ministry. Those who volunteer to serve the church will continue to serve longer, better, and with greater personal satisfaction if they are well cared for. We suggest that you focus attention on four considerations and regularly evaluate how well you are following them:

1. *Are you providing continuing education for volunteers?* Their responsibilities are large and public. And the church has so many crosscurrents of opinion and viewpoint about worship today that the work of worship leaders is more complex than in past eras. Many of these volunteers have probably had little formal training in the principles and issues of Christian worship. Consequently, they may often feel extended beyond their comfort zone. The church will serve them and their work well if it provides regular opportunities to study and grow in this field. Hillcrest Church in Hudsonville, Michigan, always included a half-hour study session at the beginning of every monthly worship committee meeting. It gave us the opportunity to learn and grow together. It provided a setting in which those of us

---

Questions for Team Care

1. Are we providing enough continuing education?
2. Are we providing adequate resources?
3. Are our meetings productive?
4. Are assignments made clearly?

It would be good for each group to ask these self-evaluative questions every few months, so that time spent together can be satisfying and productive.

---

on staff could give instruction on matters that might not otherwise be addressed. We selected good articles from publications and distributed them ahead of time. We studied our way through our denomination's official report on worship in the church. We chose sections from books on worship. True, agendas are often full, and it would have been easy to say, "We don't have time for that tonight." But we made study a priority, and the committee members agreed that it was time well spent.

2. *Are you providing adequate resources for them?* Work cannot be done well without adequate tools. Therefore, the parish that expects worship planners to work well must be willing to invest in good resources. Many new or recent books and hymnals are available. We may neither ignore them nor embrace them all. Worship leaders will do well to select and keep on hand a wide variety of the best ones to supplement the resources that are ordinarily used— including lectionary resources, liturgy resources, and books on drama. Congregations can subscribe to the best journals in the field. In addition, the church should make funds available for team members to attend conferences and workshops on worship. The church that hands the large task of worship planning to a team backs up that request with integrity when it provides the necessary resources.

3. *Are your meetings productive?* The hard question about the quality of our meetings must be asked. Meetings that drag, wander aimlessly, and end without significant accomplishments are frustrating and demoralizing. Perhaps more people have lost heart in their tasks because of boring or unproductive meetings than for any other

reason. Whatever the name of the group or the type of meeting, effective meetings include:

- a clear purpose,
- an emphasis on prayer for God's direction in planning,
- an agenda that all receive ahead of time for their own preparation,
- completion of all tasks assigned at the last meeting,
- an atmosphere in which all can participate and know they will be heard,
- group movement toward decisions and actions, and
- efficient use of time.

4. *Are assignments clear?* The work of worship planning cannot be completed in a group meeting. Group members will need to complete tasks between meetings. However, tasks must be clearly spelled out so that members do not leave the meeting without understanding what is expected of them. The presiding officer should state what the task is, what will be required to complete the task, who is responsible for doing it, and when it should be completed. It is important to note that the convener is the one responsible for such assignments. She or he must be sure the assignments are clear and made gently and considerately.

WHEN IT COMES TOGETHER

Marge sat in a worship service last Sunday morning. It wasn't easy for her to go because she had had a difficult week. She had been anxious about the welfare of her married daughter, and when she expressed her feelings to her daughter, the two of them had harsh words. When Sunday morning came, she was tired. It would have been easy to stay home. But she felt the need to worship and went to church, somewhat reluctantly, hoping that it would be good for her.

When she arrived, she was greeted warmly by several friends and courteously escorted to her seat by an usher. She found the music stirring. Some of the readings and prayers seemed to speak especially to her needs. She began to feel less stressed and to look upward. The week had involved far too much looking down, she thought. More and more she began to regard her stresses differently, and by the time she left, she realized that she had encountered God. She had prayed, given testimony to her faith in song, and received encouragement from God's Word. She thanked the pastor at the close of the service and left with a new spirit in her heart.

What she didn't know—and what the pastor could have told her but didn't—was that this worship service that brought her before God had involved the work and prayers of many people behind the scenes. Marge never thought of the choir rehearsal, the organist's preparations, the careful selection of songs, the way others had labored over the litany, the work required to sew the new banner that graced the sanctuary, and the pastor's earnest efforts to find the right words for the prayer. She never thought of those things. But they were all there. And all of these preparations became tools in the hands of the Spirit for good worship that day.

WORSHIP RESOURCE BANK SURVEY (SAMPLE)

The worship planning team of our congregation aims to include laypeople in worship leadership. We want to practice the Reformation principle of the priesthood of all believers. Worship is not done for the people, as though they were spectators, but *by* the people of God as their corporate offering of adoration and praise to him.

We solicit volunteers, young and old, male and female, who are willing to see this participation as part of their ministry to the body of Christ. A commitment should be made for an entire year, and all volunteers will serve under the supervision of the worship planning team.

Since we begin with a new list each season, please note that those who signed up last year must sign up again. If more than one person is using this form, please write your names in to identify which person is volunteering for which tasks.

If you have questions, or if you desire a copy of our worship guidelines, please read the brochure "Worship Life" in our literature rack, or speak to the pastor or the director of music.

Your Name _____

Liturgy

Please check your area of interest. You may indicate multiple areas of involvement.

☐ I'd be willing to participate in readings, litanies, and Scripture reading.

☐ I'd be willing to lead in readings and prayers with the Advent candles this season.

☐ I'd be willing to participate in a dramatized Scripture reading for worship.

☐ I'd be willing to coach an occasional Scripture drama group.

☐ I'd be willing to lead in prayer.

☐ I'd be willing to offer a children's message.

Music

Vocal

☐ I'd be willing to participate as a soloist (circle the appropriate vocal range)

soprano   alto   tenor   bass

    ☐ I'd be willing to participate as part of a theme choir, such as a family choir, women's group, men's group, or couples ensemble.

Instrumental

    ☐ I'd be interested in serving as an accompanist or providing an offertory.

    ☐ I'd like to be considered for the bell choir as openings become available.

    ☐ I'm willing to participate in a small instrumental ensemble:

        Instrument(s) played _____

    ☐ I'm willing to serve as an instrumental soloist.

Occasional Ensembles

    ☐ I'd be willing to participate in an ensemble:

        ☐ middle-school vocal
        ☐ high-school vocal
        ☐ trumpet
        ☐ flute
        ☐ string

Music Administration

    ☐ I'd be willing to serve as a music librarian.

    ☐ I'd be willing to serve as a music task force member.

LETTER TO A WORSHIP PLANNING VOLUNTEER (SAMPLE)

Dear Friend:

We are pleased that you have expressed a willingness to join with others in planning worship for our congregation. We give thanks to God for people like you who love to worship and who are committed to help others do it well! We give you a hearty welcome!

As we're sure you have noticed, worship is at the heart of our life in this congregation. We love to worship, we want our worship to be vital and Spirit filled, and we offer it to honor our Lord. Planning worship is not an easy task, but it is a rich privilege that is enormously satisfying. I'm sure that your own love of worship has led you to make yourself available for this ministry, and that your love for this congregation leads you in your desire to serve.

In preparation for your work, we ask you to read the vision statement about worship written for our congregation. In that statement we express our conviction that our worship life is primary among all the ministries of this congregation. It is in worship that we are formed spiritually. God is the One who is always to be at the center of our worship, and you'll discover that this conviction guides all our planning. We cannot boast that our worship services are perfect, but we are moved by the conviction that we must offer nothing less than our best to our glorious Lord, and we encourage you to approach this work in the same spirit.

As you join others in this work, we make several requests that we believe will make your role more satisfying and productive.

1. Worship faithfully, publicly and privately, for only as you worship will you be able to aid others in worship.
2. Continue to read and study in the area of worship. Much literature in this field is available to us today, and from time to time we'll make suggestions about what to study and read. As you grow, you will be able to help others.
3. Make a covenant with us to participate fully in our planning meetings. We meet together on the third Tuesday of each month, but there will be other assignments and small-group meetings in between that you may have to attend. Make these a priority in your scheduling.

4. Enter into a covenant with us to carry out all assignments given to you and to complete them thoughtfully and in a timely manner, with a prayer that the Spirit of God will guide you.
5. Be a full team member with us. We like to think of ourselves as a group of disciples who are called by Christ to plan the weekly worship of the church. We love, respect, and listen to one another. Our own healthy relationships will certainly serve to shape the kind of worship we plan for the congregation.

If at any time you have questions about our work and our policies, please feel free to raise your concerns with any one of us. We're committed to listen, to help, and to work with one another.

It is our prayer that you will find this role of service satisfying and that you will sense that there is no holier time of the week than the hour when God's children come into his presence in worship. Our prayers are with you.

The Worship Committee

CHAPTER 2

STRUCTURING THE PLANNING PROCESS

Members of Hillcrest Church knew they would soon face a major decision. Their morning worship service was overflowing. They were in a growing community and could expect continued growth. The first question: Should they go to two morning worship services? The answer to that one seemed obvious. But the next question soon followed it: Should the services be identical or different? Decision-makers sensed that the answer they gave to that question would shape the congregation long into the future and that they could not afford to answer it quickly or without adequate research and reflection.

The worship committee identified 11 churches within 35 miles that had dealt with this question and had handled it in various ways. The committee agreed to divide these churches among themselves, to visit them, and to learn from the experiences of each church.

After two months they returned to the subject, shared what they had learned, and drew conclusions about the method they believed would be best for Hillcrest Church. They documented their conclusion with data from their research and sent the proposal as a recommendation to the full church board for its consideration and adoption. The board found the documentation of their research convincing, approved the committee recommendation, and informed the congregation of their decision, the reasons for it, and the committee's research methods. With such a healthy process, it was easy for the congregation to trust the decision of the church board on the matter.

The theme of the worship service at Peace Church was centered on God's act of giving his law to his people at Mount Sinai as a guide for their new life in a new land. When the worship sheet was printed, the staff realized that the director of the children's choir had inserted a children's anthem, whose text named such items as "apple-red happiness, popcorn cheerfulness, cinnamon singin' inside, peppermint energy, and gumdrop holidays," and implied that these things come to us when we are Christians. Many were upset. They felt the song may have been appropriate in a Sunday school setting, or for vacation Bible school, but not for public worship. Significant dissonance was evident between the theme of the song and the theme of the service.

Whose responsibility was it to screen music for services? Did all music leaders have the right to include the songs they wanted? Should the pastor have questioned the choice? Should music selections have been reviewed first by the planning team? Or didn't it matter?

Larry and his wife had not been happy with the worship in their church for some time. They had values and viewpoints that differed from those of the pastor, the director of music, and the worship committee on matters of worship. After conversations with a number of his like-minded friends, Larry, a member of the church board, decided to bring up the matter at the next board meeting. He asked for the floor, voiced his complaints, and said he was convinced that the worship life of the church needed some evaluation and revision.

During the meeting the pastor tried to explain that the worship life of the congregation was under the supervision of a 10-member worship committee that reported to the congregation's board of elders, not to the church board that was hearing these complaints. The pastor's words fell on deaf ears. The presiding officer agreed that the matter should be explored, that Larry and others should have the right to voice their complaints at the next meeting of the church board, and that the entire worship committee should be present to respond to the complaints. That scheduled interview produced little insight, much anguish, and a great deal of pain. The worship committee members felt as though they had been put on trial.

What went wrong? Should such a discussion have taken place in the meeting of a group that was not responsible for worship supervision? What should the presiding officer have done?

"Who is in charge?" is a question that circulates through the worship life of the church. Someone must be in charge. The buck has to stop somewhere. If no one is in charge, then most people can assume that *they* are in charge, and anarchy often results. Confusion arises, and feelings can easily be hurt. Only when the lines of responsibility are clearly drawn will collaboration occur smoothly.

In this chapter we address this question. Congregations have multiple levels of decision making. We'll identify some of those levels and identify a variety of models of supervision used by churches. At the end of this chapter you will find sample guidelines for various groups.

TWO TIERS OF SUPERVISION

Though worship planning in one congregation may differ significantly from that in another congregation, supervision is generally needed on two major levels—establishing vision and policy, and planning worship.

Establishing Vision and Policy

A church without clearly established policies for its worship life is like a ship without a rudder, or a traveler without a map. Some policies deal with the logistics and outward practices of worship: At what time will worship services be held? Where will they be held? How many services will we have? But other policies involve theological issues that lie at the very heart of worship: What is our understanding of the nature of worship? What theological and biblical principles will guide our worship life? What style of worship should mark this congregation? In what way and how often will Holy Communion (the Lord's Supper) be celebrated in our services? What criteria will guide us in making these determinations?

We address the matter of formulating a worship statement for your congregation in chapter 3. There we explore the importance of having a well-formulated statement to guide all those who serve in the worship life of the church. Note that in most denominations, establishing policy is the responsibility of the governing board of the congregation. Nearly all Protestant congregations have an elected or appointed governing board that provides overall supervision for the life of the congregation. The church body's constitution, by-laws, or church order usually specify the nature, size, and function of such a body. For instance, the Constitution of the Evangelical Lutheran Church in America says:

> The Congregation Council shall have general oversight of the life and activities of this congregation, and in particular its worship life, to the end that everything be done in accordance with the Word of God and the faith and practice of the Evangelical Lutheran Church in America [C12.04].

The Church Order of the Christian Reformed Church in North America says, "The consistory [i.e., elders] shall regulate the worship services" (Art. 52a). This body is the representative group that is ultimately responsible for the life of the congregation and the formulation of its policies. In some churches board members might be called trustees, elders, parish commissioners, governors, or council members.

The Work of Planning

The other area requiring supervision involves the work of worship planning. The weekly worship services of the congregation must reflect the policies established by the church board. Planning work is never finished and has become more complex than it was a generation ago. Who sets up the long-range worship calendar for the church? Who determines how the seasons of the church will shape its worship life? Who designs the actual services, selects the songs, and puts all the pieces of the puzzle together so that on Sunday morning all is ready? These tasks are intensive and require careful attention by people who are deeply committed to worship. At a minimum, most churches will hold 52 worship services a year. Others, however, that have morning and evening worship, or midweek services and special worship events, may have more than 100 to plan! That's a large task, one requiring people who are able to meet regularly and invest a significant amount of time to worship planning.

The church board responsible for establishing policy will not be able to involve itself in the planning process. It almost always delegates the work to others who are able to meet more frequently. We address the methodologies and strategies of worship planning in chapters 4 and 5. Note that in most congregations several tiers of people receive delegated tasks.

A worship committee is usually appointed, or at least approved by the church board, to oversee the worship life of the congregation on behalf of the church board. Membership usually ranges from six to 12 members, with a balance of male and female, representing various age groups in the congregation. Most churches make such appointments for a specific term, usually two or three years, ensuring a balance of healthy continuity and fresh insight. Some churches allow members to remain on the committee for an indeterminate period of time if they are serving well, and others will allow a certain number of one-year extensions to the three-year term. In all cases it is assumed that the pastor and the director of music (or a practicing musician) are permanent members of the committee.

Since this group usually meets monthly at most, it cannot engage in weekly worship planning. So the worship committee delegates the planning responsibilities to a worship planning team that meets at least weekly to do the work of constructing the worship services. But even a worship planning team, meeting weekly, finds that many matters still need attention between meetings. Therefore, certain people, either volunteer or staff, are given the responsibility for details.

We will explore various models for planning, but nearly all defined models are built around this basic tiered structure:

- A governing board that is responsible for overall worship policy
- A worship committee that oversees the worship life of the church
- A worship planning team that carries out basic work of creating worship services from week to week
- A few people, volunteer or staff, who oversee the details on an ongoing basis

This structure will need to be varied or modified to fit the situation of each congregation. Churches within a more liturgical tradition, in which quite a few matters of worship are "set," may require fewer tiers. Smaller churches may not find all the tiers helpful, or may find them overlapping.

A congregation must make sure that people in the various tiers communicate regularly and clearly with one another. The worship committee should certainly include at least one member of the church governing board so that information and recommendations can be conveyed back and forth. Similarly, the worship planning teams will have liaisons to the worship committee so that all can stay informed of each other's activities and concerns.

MODELS FOR WEEKLY PLANNING

We've had contact with many churches from a variety of denominations about their worship-planning models. We have found great variety, but four general models. The size, culture, and history of a congregation influence which model it selects for its worship planning. There is room for variety, and each congregation should consider the criteria it will use when selecting a model. What resources do we have available? Do we have paid staff? How many musicians do we have and with what skills? How large is our congregation? To what practices of worship planning has the congregation grown accustomed? How well are they working?

Staff-Driven Planning

The staff-driven model for planning is used most often in larger churches, especially when a full-time staff position is devoted to music. The church board will generally continue to be responsible for overall policy in the worship life of the church, and a worship committee may function to implement that policy; but both have little involvement on a week-to-week basis. That work is delegated to staff members. Where there is more than one preaching pastor, ordinarily the pastor who will preach in a service participates in the planning for that service. The staff members have autonomy within board policy. Their position is a privileged one. At LaGrave Christian Reformed Church, a large congregation in Grand Rapids, Michigan, the minister of preaching and the minister of music usually meet on Tuesday afternoons for weekly planning. In addition, the minister of music meets with the chancel choir director to coordinate the worship planning. At St. Matthew's Church, a Lutheran congregation in Perkasie, Pennsylvania, the pastor and the director of music plan all worship services together. The pastor selects the texts from the Revised Common Lectionary and formulates his theme for the day. The director of music receives that information to plan the music for each service. They select hymns together.

This model assumes that the church has paid staff members who have the time to invest in planning, adequate authorization from others to make all the necessary decisions, and a high level of trust from all. This model is efficient, but staff members will probably want to solicit input from a broad range of members for the planning process.

Pastor and Musician Team

Whereas the previous model assumes that worship planners are paid staff members, in this model we find a pastor who is working with a musician in a collaborative partnership, though no staff position is involved. The musician may well be a paid organist or pianist, who in addition has volunteered for the task of worship planning. The pastor most often takes the primary role, establishing the worship schedule, including major events and the theme of each service. The musician assists the pastor in crafting the rest of the worship service around the sermon and theme. For instance, a small congregation has a pastor who is serving the members well, but his time and ability to design meaningful liturgies is somewhat limited. The organist has volunteered to work with the pastor on worship planning. They meet each Wednesday morning, and the worship service is the product of their joint efforts. The pastor is grateful for the assistance that comes from someone who sees planning efforts as a gift to the congregation.

Such an arrangement is ideal for a small congregation with fewer resources. It is important, however, that the two people are compatible in their understanding of worship and able to work together. The challenge, however, is that the musician is often untrained in matters of worship and may not have the background to make some decisions. Therefore, the congregation would be wise to provide an educational allowance for training and encourage the pastor to mentor the volunteer. At the same time, since pastors are often insufficiently trained in the area of music, provisions should be made for music training for the pastor, and perhaps the musician could also serve as a mentor to the pastor. The long-term benefit to the congregation is well worth the effort invested.

Multiple Planning Teams

A third model makes use of multiple planning teams. These teams are composed of members of the congregation who share responsibility for worship planning, usually for a limited period of time. The worship committee serves as a constant in this model, overseeing the entire worship life of the church, while the pastor serves as the key person in selecting the Scripture texts and themes for worship. The pastor is involved in the work of each team so that all are kept well informed, though the degree of the pastor's involvement may be determined by schedule and desire. These teams, which may range from two to six people, work with the pastor or the pastor's material, under the supervision of the worship committee, to construct the services of worship for the weeks assigned to them.

In our contacts and conversations with churches we found five methods of arranging these teams:

1. *Weekly teams.* Each week a different team of planners is responsible, and the pastor works with each team. The size of a congregation, and the number of volunteers available to serve, will determine how workable this model is. If, for instance, there are four weekly planning teams, then each will be responsible for one week of the month. At Loop Christian Ministries of Chicago the members of the worship committee attend monthly meetings and discuss overall issues and advance planning, but each member takes individual responsibility for preparing and leading the liturgy as often as every six weeks.

2. *Monthly teams.* Some believe that weekly teams do not provide enough continuity. If a different team plans the service each week, the worship services from one week to another may be very different in tone. Consequently, many churches prefer to assign an entire month to a team. When the month is finished, team members take a rest until their month comes up again.

3. *Rotating teams.* We've found other churches that are concerned about the work that worship planning involves and don't want anyone to be overloaded or to lose freshness. So they distribute the planning among multiple teams, but not on the basis of weeks, months, or seasons. These teams are assigned their Sundays on the basis of a regular rotation for a certain number of weeks or months, depending on how many teams are available.

4. *Seasonal Teams.* Other churches, particularly those that pay close attention to the Christian year, prefer that a planning team focus on a season of the church year. Separate planning teams will be organized for Advent, Lent, Eastertide, and so on. This planning

team will be able to focus all its research and efforts on its assigned season. Such a team will likely be composed of members who have expertise and interest in the season assigned.

5. *Sectional teams.* Instead of asking a planning team to take responsibility for an entire worship service, some congregations have chosen to designate separate planning teams for specific parts of the worship service. One team may specialize in developing the service of confession; another team focuses its efforts on writing litanies and prayers; yet another will concentrate on the role of children in the service, or the sacraments; another might focus on the music. Each of these teams has been given the themes and Scripture readings for the service so that the content will be consistent in theme. One lay planner or the pastor will take all the components and integrate them into an order of service.

The possibilities are limited only by circumstance and imagination. We believe a congregation's worship life will be richer when more people are involved in planning. However, bringing in more people presents challenges.

What about consistency and flow of information? Teams must communicate clearly and fully with one another. Will all of the participants have adequate training in matters of worship? It would be good for teams to take time to study worship to foster their own continued growth. And congregations would be wise to provide for adequate resources and educational opportunities for team members.

Another issue is the compatibility of those who work together. Do they have the same "worship DNA," or will each team potentially become a nest of conflict and power struggles? Will separate teams develop competing identities, with each becoming a voice for a faction of the congregation? When team members are appointed, people's working styles, personalities, and knowledge of worship should be factored in.

Staff and Committee Partnership

We have found this model mainly in larger churches where a paid staff works closely with a committee in shaping the worship life of the church. This model is a hybrid of the first two. The committee—in this case the

---

Four Common Models for Worship-Planning Ministries

1. Staff-driven planning
2. Pastor and musician team
3. Multiple planning teams
4. Staff and committee partnership

---

worship committee—meets regularly to evaluate past worship services, brainstorm for future services, and approve the main seasonal worship calendar. Yet committee members leave the weekly planning and construction of worship in the hands of staff. This arrangement requires a healthy flow of information and ideas between committee and staff, and a healthy level of trust in those who are handed the tasks of weekly planning. This arrangement may also include a variety of task forces or subcommittees for other areas of work.

At Hillcrest Church, a Christian Reformed congregation in Hudsonville, Michigan, the worship committee of 10 members meets each month for a full evening to study issues of worship, to review and evaluate the past month's worship, to review and contribute ideas for future services, and to receive reports and recommendations from its task forces. However, the work of designing worship services for each Sunday is left completely in the hands of the senior pastor and the director of music, who call on the task forces for assistance.

Such an arrangement usually provides for a clear understanding of the role of both the council and staff members and allows for great efficiency. A monthly committee meeting provides a healthy arena for discussion, evaluation, brainstorming, and support. Yet, the work of putting worship together each week is in the hands of those who have developed expertise in the area. This arrangement allows staff members to receive healthy feedback and input from a broader range of people. Otherwise, the staff members who do the planning can become too far removed from the members of the congregation and their needs. This model works best when committee members are candid and staff members are not defensive.

Many modifications can be made within these four common models, depending on the local needs and resources of each congregation. Such decisions should be made with due consideration for gaining the broadest possible support within the leadership of the congregation. We suggest these criteria in making your choice:

- What is the history of worship planning of your congregation and how has that shaped what is expected in planning today?
- What are the desires, expectations, and interests of the (senior) pastor? Is he or she knowledgeable in matters of worship and music? Creative? Open to assistance and collaboration with others?
- Does your church have other staff members who should be involved, who desire to be involved, and who have the necessary knowledge and expertise?
- Are other gifted and knowledgeable members of the congregation able to serve well with the pastor in weekly worship planning? Are they respected and trusted by others in the congregation?
- Does your congregation have others who are willing and able to assist in either short-term or long-term planning?
- How many musicians are available in your congregation? Can one serve as mentor for the others?
- Are the current relationships between the pastor and musician(s) marked by trust and respect, making it possible for them to work together?
- Does your congregation have an appointed worship committee? How many members? For how long a term do they serve? What role do they desire in the worship life of the church?

Such considerations will affect which model will serve most effectively in your situation. For instance, one church planned to use a member of the congregation who had organizational skills to coordinate worship. However, decision-makers soon discovered that the task required much more than organizational skills; they realized they needed someone with musical ability. They then moved toward the pastor-musician model. Another congregation gave all the worship planning responsibilities to two gifted staff members but learned over a period of time that these two were in danger of burning out unless they received more assistance from others. So the church moved toward the staff and committee partnership model. In another parish a large number of eager planners with many viewpoints created chaos, prompting a move toward a more staff-driven model. Yet as we have said, all models require effective communication.

Supplementary Teams

Once you have determined your model and adapted it to your situation, other tasks and levels of participants become involved. A well-rounded worship life requires more than words and music. Many disciplines and skills are needed. Perhaps you include lay readers, prayer leaders, liturgical dancers, musical ensembles, visual artists who prepare the worship space, and coordinators of children's activities. You will also need the help of people behind the scenes preparing worship bulletins; cleaning and maintaining the worship space; providing slides, video, and PowerPoint materials; and managing the sound equipment. Therefore, those who plan worship will need to draw on the gifts and expertise of others in a wide variety of fields.

These are all "supplementary teams." At Hillcrest Church we worked with the director of the children's ministry, the directors of children's choirs, coordinator for instrumentalists, artists who created banners, groups of lay readers, a coach for those who prepared Scripture dramas, a team responsible for the sacraments, an office staff, custodians, and others.

You can see how our work was organized in the chart on page 47, with an alternate chart provided on page 48. The first chart shows the team members and their interrelationships at Hillcrest Church. You will notice that the church board (the elders) is the ruling body at the center. The primary planners are the senior pastor, the director of music, and the worship committee. The secondary participants who work with them are in the next wider circle. The large number of assistants for other tasks is found in the outermost circle.

Webster Grove Christian Church in Baldwin, Missouri, has organized a set-up team, a put-away team, a reach-out team, a music team, a worship leadership team, and a pastoral team (Tim and Kathy Carson, *So You're Thinking about Contemporary Worship* [St. Louis: Chalice Press, 1997], 20ff.). Robert Webber of Northern Theological Seminary in Lombard, Illinois, a noted author on worship issues, writes about establishing teams for music

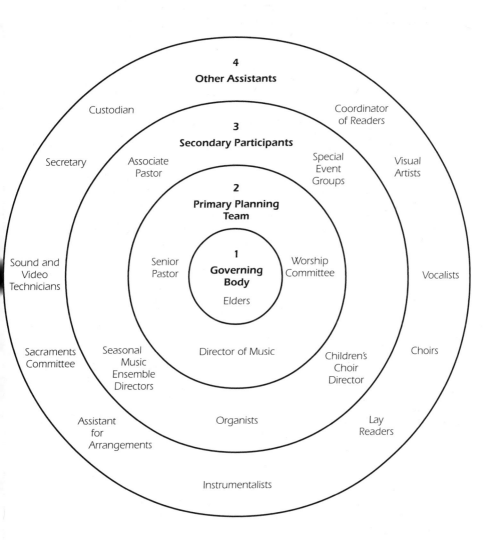

Chart of Worship Planning Team Members

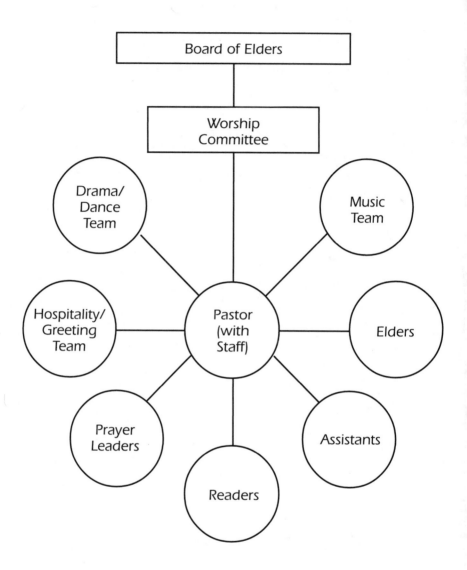

Alternative Chart of Worship Planning Team Members

and the arts, one for leadership, and another responsible for "housekeeping," which includes all technical matters—the bulletins, hospitality, preparation for communion, and so forth (Webber, *Planning for Blended Worship* [Nashville: Abingdon, 1998], 198-199). The number of teams you have, their structure, and their size should be shaped by the needs of your congregation. Creative organization is needed here.

STEPS IN THE PLANNING PROCESS

Now that we have explored the basic structure of a congregation and identified who might be responsible at various levels, let's turn our attention to the elements of the planning process. Careful planning is a complex enterprise. Vital worship will take place when all the pieces of the planning puzzle are put together well.

Before explaining the steps, we must acknowledge the role of the Holy Spirit and prayer in worship planning. Whatever structure we have outlined for worship will be empty unless the Holy Spirit fills it with his blessing. Worship planning may not be a totally human effort, for none of us possess sufficient wisdom and discernment within ourselves alone. We assume, therefore, that worship planners faithfully call on the Holy Spirit.

1. Selecting the Seasonal Calendar

Worship planners must ask how they will structure their season of worship. What considerations and events will determine where emphases will be placed? Will we follow a September-through-May program calendar? Or the annual January-through-December calendar? Or the secular calendar of national events and "greeting card" days? Or will we use the Christian calendar, in which the year begins with Advent and is completed with the season after Pentecost, or "Ordinary time," and Christ the King Sunday? We explore this matter further in chapter 4, but let us just note here that this determination is the first step in the planning process.

2. Designing Seasonal Units

Whether or not you plan to follow a traditional church-year calendar, you will probably observe at least some seasons and days of the church year.

Planners will want to begin their work by identifying those observances. For example, the four weeks of Advent are a unit. The six weeks of Lent are another unit. Holy Week deserves special attention. Will we have a Christmas candlelight service? How about Maundy Thursday and Good Friday? What will Easter involve? Ascension Day? Pentecost?

3. Brainstorming Major Events

Once the seasonal calendar has been established, other major events in worship must be considered. These might include mission emphasis, stewardship month, and a congregational anniversary. Identify these, brainstorm about them, and begin to think of who will carry extra responsibilities to plan for them. Will we observe World Communion Sunday? Thanksgiving Day? Perhaps there are events unique to the life of your congregation that need to be included. Some churches have appointed a "special events" team for each of these major events. For instance, a few members from the stewardship committee can be appointed, along with a few experienced worship planners, to plan for a time of stewardship emphasis. Others will appoint one planning team for all special events. Be sure that careful communication flows between these groups and other worship planners.

4. Constructing the Weekly Service

Every week at least one worship service needs to be constructed, and Sundays seem to come along rapidly! It is advantageous to have multiple weekly services in various stages of preparation at any given time. We explore this process in chapter 5, but here we observe that weekly planning requires that all information needed on the theme of each service is available, that all planners have done their "homework," and that all the pieces are ready to be put together to create an integrated whole. Whatever the style of worship, planners must take care that this effort has been bathed in a prayer for the Holy Spirit's blessing so that this service can be a rich encounter between God and his children.

5. Making Final Preparations

What is created in the weekly planning session is still private. It's on a computer screen, or in rough draft on sheets of paper. Now it must take on a

---

Checklist for Putting the Pieces Together

1. Selecting the seasonal calendar
2. Designing seasonal units
3. Brainstorming major events
4. Constructing the weekly service
5. Making final preparations
6. Doing a pre-worship walk-through
7. Making a post-service review
8. Conducting a formal evaluation

---

more public form so that others can participate. Others must be brought into the plan—those who direct groups, coach leaders, arrange rehearsals, prepare projection slides and other visuals, secure the necessary copyright permissions, and prepare readable and understandable printed worship folders. All these are valuable steps and need to be done well.

6. Doing the Worship Walk-Through

When the time for worship arrives on Sunday, those who lead the service will experience their share of anxiety and jitters. No wonder! Leading in worship is a holy privilege. These normal anxieties will become exaggerated if leaders are not sure of their roles, or are afraid that something essential has escaped their attention. While a dress rehearsal like the one staged by a drama team is not necessary, last-minute "walk-throughs" are helpful. As pastor and musician, we always took a short time on Saturday morning to go carefully through the service to look for needed transitions, potential difficulties, and items needing more careful attention. Then before the service began on Sunday, we gathered all the participants for one last look at the service to be sure that everyone was clear about his or her role, the necessary cues, and any last-minute questions. After all was reviewed, we had a time of prayer, asking that the Lord would give a fullness of his Spirit while we worshiped him.

7. Making a Post-Service Review

As those who had the primary role in planning and leading the service, we felt it was necessary to gather briefly, shortly after the time of worship, to review it. While we were well aware of the fact that we were too close to conduct any kind of objective evaluation, we believe that the work of worship is not done when the service is ended. We knew that a full review would be done later with others, but for now we needed to ask ourselves some questions: Did we select songs the worshipers were able to sing well? What was the mood and spirit of the congregation? Were there any glaring omissions? What distractions did we encounter? Where did God seem to break through most clearly? This can be only a preliminary review, but a necessary one, for these are the kinds of reflections that can easily be lost after a few days.

8. Conducting a Formal Evaluation

At the next monthly worship committee meeting a more formal and objective evaluation of the worship is conducted. We've done this evaluation on a regular basis, but we have discovered that many others do not, though they sense it ought to be done. We discuss the entire evaluation process further in chapter 6. We believe that a healthy and vital worship life means asking hard questions so that we may learn what best helps people to encounter God. Evaluation requires a willingness to learn from past mistakes so as not to repeat them.

We have now put together two major parts of the process of worship planning—exploring four models for carrying out such planning, and an eight-step process that is compatible with all four models. We encourage you to make whatever adaptations are necessary in your congregation.

THE WORK OF THE COMMITTEE

Each of the models for planning assumes that a worship committee is in place, whatever name it may be given. We believe that each congregation should have a standing worship committee that exercises oversight of the worship life of the congregation on behalf of the governing board. Members are appointed or approved by the governing board. Their term of appointment is for a stated number of years, usually two or three.

Members of the committee should be committed to the worship life of the church, knowledgeable about worship and music, committed to growing, and demonstrably committed in a healthy way to the welfare of the congregation. When appointments are made, the governing board should also take two other factors into consideration: The committee should be representative of the make up of the congregation, representing various ethnic groups in the congregation, as well as a balance of male and female, old and young. And those who are appointed to this committee should be a compatible group so that its members will be able to function together smoothly and collaboratively. The members should share a common worship "DNA"—that is, a common worship perspective, so that meetings do not become a hotbed for arguments and divisiveness. In *Designing Worship Teams,* Cathy Townley says:

> Actors try to discover the DNA of the character they're portraying. How the character looks, acts, feels, tastes, smells, and sounds—what makes the person tick—make him real to both the actor and, ultimately, the audience. Worship teams and other bodies of believers also have godly DNA that must be discovered and then articulated, for it is what makes God real in their own lives and others' lives in which God would be revealed [Nashville: Abingdon, 2002, 69].

Tim and Kathy Carson's suggestion in *So You're Thinking about Contemporary Worship* (St. Louis: Chalice Press, 1997, 20) that this committee should always meet around a round table has more than practical significance. It also has theological implications because it symbolizes the unity of mind, heart, and function that should characterize this group.

Samples of the guidelines that shape the tasks of this committee are included at the end of this chapter (see page 59). Though there is room for variation, certain common responsibilities are usually considered:

1. *Education.* A task as far-reaching as worship planning requires committee members who take seriously their own learning and growth. An effective committee will want to spend time in study and discussion about worship and its issues, and group members should encourage the congregation to do the same. Appendix A, "Resources for Group Study" (page 177), suggests some helpful materials.

2. *Policy.* While the governing board of the congregation sets ultimate policy for the life of the congregation in accordance with the constitution or bylaws of the denomination, the worship committee

---

Common Worship Committee Responsibilities

1. Education
2. Policy
3. Budgeting
4. Coordination
5. Brainstorming
6. Appointments
7. Evaluation

---

is responsible for knowing and understanding these policies. It takes the lead in implementing them and, when necessary, recommends any needed modifications. Recall that in the opening of this chapter Hillcrest Church dealt smoothly with a major policy decision because the task of each body was clearly understood and accepted. Conversely, in the third anecdote, a worship committee was treated unfairly when policy was not followed.

3. *Budgeting.* The worship life of a congregation will incur certain expenses. Each year the committee should study worship-related needs, determine what resources should be purchased, and prepare a proposed budget. Similarly, this committee is responsible for spending such funds wisely.

4. *Coordination.* As we have noted, planning and leading worship for a congregation can involve a large number of individuals and groups. The committee ultimately must provide for their coordination. Usually committee members will serve as liaisons to key teams and people to keep them informed. They can also relay information back to the committee as a whole. Often this work is delegated to a worship coordinator. Peace Church, in one opening illustration in this chapter, could have avoided many of the hard feelings that erupted if better coordination had been provided.

5. *Brainstorming.* The committee will need to turn itself into a think tank that develops creative ideas about the church's worship life or a particular church season. Such sessions can revitalize worship, and motivate those charged with seasonal and weekly worship planning.

6. *Appointments.* Someone must be given the authority to appoint, hire, or dismiss pianists, organists, and directors, though each congregation may assign this responsibility differently. If a staff

person has this task, the committee can serve as a sounding board when decisions are to be made.

7. *Evaluation.* Though most worshipers do their own private evaluations of each service, and the primary worship leaders are encouraged to do a post-service review, the worship committee's place in the life of the church seems to make it the logical group to conduct a formal evaluation of the congregation's worship life. Such evaluations can be done monthly, or less often, but they should be done with candor, kindness, and commitment to the worship life of the church.

The Work of the Planning Team

The work of a planning team will be somewhat different from that of the standing worship committee. The planning team is charged with crafting specific services of worship. Earlier in this chapter we indicated that a worship planning team may take a number of different forms. Whatever its assignment, the work will usually include certain common elements, with each step building on the previous one. These steps will normally include:

- Receiving information from the pastor about sermons, sermon series, Scripture readings, and themes selected for future weeks and months
- Reviewing the season of the church year and the theme of the season the team is planning
- Receiving from the director of music anthems that have been selected and are being rehearsed
- Clarifying the theme of the service
- Determining the pattern and the flow of this service
- Determining the elements of worship the liturgy will include
- Selecting hymns and songs for the service
- Selecting or writing litanies, responsive readings, dramas, and so forth
- Placing the ensemble and choral music within the service
- Recruiting the leaders who will participate in the service
- Planning for rehearsals with participants
- Preparing a readable order of service for the secretary who will put it into print

None of this work can be done without effective meetings. We all have felt the frustration of attending unproductive meetings. The convener of the meeting should observe certain guidelines to ensure a productive and satisfying work session. Before the meeting he or she should prepare a clear agenda and distribute it so that all members may prepare in advance. Begin with a devotional period to set the meeting's spiritual tone. Business can be conducted most fairly if team members have a general awareness of the guidelines of parliamentary procedure, though the culture of each congregation will determine how rigorously Robert's Rules, or other meeting procedures, are enforced. Those who present reports or other information should be heard and respected, and all other members should have the opportunity to ask questions for clarification. Every member must be treated with respect so that all feel free to contribute their ideas and suggestions. Should a disagreement arise, an atmosphere of trust and respect will foster a setting in which the matter can be discussed and resolved. While all should be heard, the presider must continue to move the group toward decisions and actions. When these general guidelines are observed, meetings will be both productive and satisfying.

Carefully prepared agendas are essential to a well-functioning committee. The agenda should include a list of reports to be received and tasks to be accomplished in the order in which they can best be handled. At the end of this chapter you will also find sample agendas for both worship committee meetings and planning team meetings (see pages 65-66). These offer a general model and can be modified and adjusted to fit your own situation.

Learning and Growing

A vital element in the work of both worship committees and planning teams is that of their own learning and growth. Those who supervise and plan the worship services of a community need to be constantly growing in their own understanding and competence in the field. Today we deal with so many issues, some new and some old, that continual learning is more necessary than ever. We can easily be swayed by unhealthy trends and lose our direction if we do not understand the purpose and practices of worship. In addition, so many excellent resources designed to encourage our growth are available today that it would be a shame not to use them. Committee members can be invited to attend conferences and workshops, and funds should be provided for expenses. In addition, each meeting can include a time for group study. True, when meeting agendas are full and the workload is heavy, it's easy to say, "We just don't have time for a study session today!" and group study is repeatedly put off until the very idea fades in group memory.

However, we have found such times of study to be highly profitable and well worth the investment, even when some other parts of the meeting must be made more efficient. We have always tried to encourage a half-hour study session in each meeting of the worship committee and planning team. We have worked through our denomination's study of worship, *Authentic Worship in a Changing Culture*. Perhaps your denomination has a similar publication. In addition, we have selected stimulating articles from journals about worship. We have included a list of materials suggested for study in appendix A, "Resources for Group Study" (pg. 177). Members of your group should feel free to suggest study materials. A study session is usually more profitable when the members have material to read and study before arriving at the meeting.

DREAMING THE POSSIBLE

We have spelled out some of the options for worship planning structures. However, organizations do not always measure up to what we expect of them. Worship planners and leaders need patience and understanding. As we work together, we always seek to improve the quality of our structure, our work, and our relationships.

We have corresponded with a number of worship planners about their experiences, and you have seen some of their comments in this chapter. But in addition to asking them what is happening in their congregation, we asked them about their dreams and the developments they would *like to see* happening. Some of their comments can give us good direction. Imagine that we have gathered them in one room and you are given the opportunity to hear them express their dreams and desires.

You would hear some busy volunteers wishing for a staff person who could coordinate their work better. And then you'd hear a part-time staff person wanting to devote more time to worship planning. Another staff person wishes there were more subcommittees or task forces to assist. Another, fresh from a planning meeting, wishes that the group could agree more readily on a set time to meet on a regular basis, so that all could attend every meeting. One planning committee member wishes the group could receive material from the pastor further in advance so that they could plan more than a month ahead. Several would like to find some way to understand the needs of the congregation better before they begin planning worship. All agree that they need more training and education in the issues of worship. Laypeople feel they are often dealing with matters that are over their heads, and pastors would like to help them become more articulate in matters of worship. All agree that they should get beyond discussing the nuts and bolts of a worship service and focus more on the heart and soul of it, and whether the worship they plan really does encourage an encounter with God.

Imagine how enjoyable planning could be and how vital worship could become if all these dreams were realized!

SAMPLE GUIDELINES FOR WORSHIP COMMITTEES

Sample 1

1. *General Purpose.* To nurture the corporate worship life of this congregation as inspiring, celebrative, and centered on the faithful preaching of the word of God and the celebration of the sacraments.

2. *Accountability.* The committee shall report to the governing body of the church.

3. *Membership.* The committee shall consist of eight to 10 members and shall include the vice president of the council, who shall serve as chairperson; another elder; the senior pastor; the director of music; and other members of the congregation. The senior pastor and director of music shall have continuing membership on the committee.

4. *General Duties.*
   a. To plan regularly services of worship that include the proclamation of the Word, confession, praise, prayer, giving of gifts, and celebration of the sacraments.
   b. To study biblical worship regularly to carry out the committee's mandate intelligently and in an informed manner.
   c. To arrange for pulpit supply as needed.
   d. To make reports and recommendations, as necessary, to the governing body.
   e. To make budget recommendations to the finance committee.
   f. To supervise and coordinate the work of the task forces.

5. *Task Forces*
   a. An audio/video ministry to maintain and operate the sound and video system and to record all worship services.
   b. A dance ministry to create liturgical dance and prepare the dancers.
   c. A drama ministry to encourage the development of dramas based on Scripture, to coach participants, and to implement such dramas in worship.

d. A greeting ministry to identify and welcome visitors as they come to worship and to provide them with helpful information.

e. A music ministry task force to assist the director of music in supervising, scheduling, and evaluating all dimensions of the music ministry.

f. A nursery ministry to maintain and staff safe and secure nurseries during all worship services.

g. A sacrament ministry to make preparations and arrangements for baptisms and Lord's Supper celebrations.

h. A tape ministry to retain a file of all taped services and to make recordings available to borrow or purchase.

i. A hospitality ministry to greet and seat worshipers in an orderly, efficient, and pleasant manner.

j. A visual arts ministry to provide attractive and appropriate banners, flowers, and other seasonal decorations.

k. A worship planning ministry to assist worship leaders in planning selected worship services and to engage in worship evaluation.

Sample 2

1. *Scope of the Committee's Work:* This committee is responsible for all matters relating to the worship ministries of the church. Its purpose shall be to ensure that each member of the congregation is striving to:
   a. Regularly attend, participate in, and benefit from worship services.
   b. Learn what it means to worship God.
   c. Faithfully celebrate the sacraments.
   d. Establish regular times of private devotion and devotions with other believers.
2. *Composition of the Committee:* The committee shall consist of the pastor, a musician, one elder, one deacon, and at least two other members of the congregation. The members of the congregation shall be appointed for a two-year term, subject to reappointment.
3. *Duties of the Committee:*
   a. To plan worship services that are theologically sound and spiritually uplifting.
   b. To study materials about biblical worship.
   c. To research, write, and produce materials for worship and instruction that will help members of the congregation learn more about worship and enable them to participate fully in all aspects of worship.
   d. To make regular evaluations of the quality of worship services.
   e. To invite all members of the congregation—young and old, male and female—to contribute their gifts to the worship life of the congregation.
   f. To plan liturgies for special occasions, such as professions of faith and welcome of new members, and to plan the proper setting for the celebration of the sacraments of baptism and the Lord's Supper.
   g. To report to the council on a regular basis with proposals and evaluations.
   h. To meet quarterly with other resource people to lay out long-range plans for worship during the approaching season of the church calendar.
   i. To coordinate with other committees on matters that affect worship services.

Sample 3

The Standing Worship Committee shall:

1. Study and seek to implement the principles of biblical worship.
2. Evaluate how well the worship services enable members of the congregation to worship.
3. Consider and implement changes that will enrich the congregation's celebration of the sacraments, other aspects of congregational worship, and special occasions in the church's calendar and the congregation's life.
4. Plan the worship services as follows:
   a. Plan the broad schedule of services for the year and each season within it and be ready to respond sensitively to immediate situations that significantly affect the life of the congregation. These shall include non-Sunday services such as services of prayer, Thanksgiving, etc.
   b. At quarterly planning sessions, with other meetings as necessary, lay out the long-range plans and the immediate plans for the coming seasons.
   c. Schedule and coordinate the contributions of all participants.
   d. Plan and coordinate other related aspects, such as the visual element in banners and bulletins.
5. Inform and educate the congregation to encourage a full understanding of and participation in all aspects of the worship experience.
6. Coordinate with other committees on matters affecting worship services.
7. Advise the governing body of the church regarding new liturgical practices.
8. Recommend to the ruling body of the church a yearly worship budget.

SAMPLE GUIDELINES FOR WORSHIP PLANNING TEAMS

Sample 1

The worship planning team shall function according to these guidelines:

A. *Membership:* The team will include up to six communicant members of the church. Each member of the team shall commit to a six-month term of service. No member may serve for more than three consecutive years without a break of at least one year.

B. *General Responsibilities:*
1. Plan elements of each special season of worship.
2. Assist the pastor in implementing plans for worship services.
3. Work in conjunction with the worship committee and in keeping with biblical practices and teaching.

C. *Specific Mandate:*
1. Plan worship to coordinate with the pastor's sermon themes, the season of the church year, and other events scheduled for various worship services.
2. Complete most of the planning for worship services at least three weeks before the services, such as choosing songs, finding responsive readings, choosing dramas, and recruiting people to participate in the services.
3. Work with banner designers at least two months ahead of time.
4. Meet as often as needed to complete the work.
5. Submit plans to the pastor for review and printing.
6. Review and evaluate worship services.
7. Read and study materials related to worship.
8. Present budget requests to the worship committee.

Sample 2

Each member of the worship planning team will ordinarily serve for three years with the option of an additional year, pending committee approval. Each member will:

1. Attend monthly meetings and participate in the rotating task of taking minutes during the meeting.
2. Write the liturgy and lead worship as often as every six weeks.
3. Work with the team to evaluate services, with the goal of enhancing worship.
4. Assist with whatever sanctuary arrangements are necessary for worship.
5. Serve as a greeter as worshipers arrive.
6. Study to remain familiar with worship guidelines and worship issues.

SAMPLE AGENDA FOR A WORSHIP COMMITTEE MEETING

1. *Opening devotions.*
2. *Minutes.* Review the minutes of the last meeting.
3. *Study.* A selected issue, article, or chapter is copied and attached to the agenda so that each member can read and study it before the meeting.
4. *Review.* The worship services of the past month are reviewed with each committee member raising any observations, evaluations, and suggestions.
5. *Planning.* Preliminary plans for upcoming worship services are set before the committee, and group members discuss what should be included and how to shape the services.
6. *Task force reports.* Each of the task forces (subcommittees) reports on its activities and raises any concerns that need to be addressed.
7. *Miscellaneous matters.*
8. *Prayer and adjournment.*

SAMPLE AGENDA FOR A WORSHIP PLANNING TEAM

1. Opening devotions and prayer.
2. Review the worship service(s) of the past week.
3. Identify the worship service that is the subject of this planning session.
4. Receive information from the pastor about sermon, Scriptures to be read, and themes for this service.
5. Receive information from musician(s) about the anthems being prepared.
6. Agree on the overall theme of the worship service, and express this theme in a succinct statement or sentence.
7. Each member of the planning team contributes suggestions on:
   a. Hymns and songs for the service.
   b. Litanies, responsive readings and dramas that may be needed.
   c. Other special events.
8. The group arranges the items to create the flow of the worship service and reinforce its theme.
9. The group identifies:
   a. Additional elements that need to be prepared for the service.
   b. Efforts needed to coordinate ensembles and choral groups.
   c. Readers and other leaders who need to be recruited.
   d. Copyright permissions that need to be secured.
   e. Assignment of the tasks that need to be done.
10. Preparation of the order of service for print.
11. Review of the worship services to be prepared during the next few weeks, noting any concerns that will need attention before the next planning session.
12. Prayer and adjournment.

CHAPTER 3

WRITING A CONGREGATIONAL WORSHIP STATEMENT

Susan had just sung with a women's ensemble for the morning worship service at Horizon Church. The ensemble had been active several years ago but had since disbanded. Some congregation members encouraged the women to get back together, so they sang on the first Sunday of Advent. The congregation, glad to have them lead in worship again, responded to their anthems with hearty applause. Now Susan was upset. She was happy to sing, but she thought applause in church was inappropriate and offensive. After the service she raised her concerns with several others and found that they held various opinions on applause in worship. Is there a way to reach agreement?

The worship planning team at Church of the Valley had just begun its meeting to plan worship for the next Sunday. The team had made good progress at its last meeting in setting the basic format for this service; now members were eager to select the readings and write the prayers. But their work hit a snag when Ron reported on a request received from the church's social committee that surprised them all. That committee, it seems, had been planning a Thanksgiving season potluck and was looking for ways to promote it to the congregation. So the committee had produced a drama for the worship service—an infomercial to bring the potluck to the congregation's attention. Silence followed Ron's report to the planning team. Finally, Ellen blurted out, "Good grief, what do we do with this now? Can we do this in worship?"

Word came to the planning committee of Hope Church that on the third Sunday of Lent, Derrick would sing during the service. Derrick has a strong baritone voice, and the congregation likes to hear him sing each time he returns home from college. But this time Derrick has suggested that his songs be accompanied by recorded music. This prerecorded music, he says, provides better accompaniment than the regular church accompanist, and he would not need to spend extra time rehearsing during his vacation. He will just bring the CD along with him and plug it into the sound system in the sanctuary. Hope Church has never dealt with this scenario. The planning group members like Derrick, and they like to hear him sing, but it just doesn't "feel right" to play a CD during worship. They don't know what to do. How should they decide?

Carl and Mary are thoughtful and enthusiastic members of Strong Hill Church. They are eager to encourage some of their neighbors to come to church with them. They've built a good relationship with the McFarleys next door. They know the McFarleys grew up in a church but no longer attend anywhere. After months of carefully building the friendship, Carl and Mary have broached the subject of worship with them. The McFarleys seem quite interested—at least interested in getting more information. The conversation turns to questions like: What is worship like at your church? What does worship mean? What will we find, and will we be able to understand it? Carl and Mary are delighted that the conversation has progressed to this point, but they are uncertain how to explain worship at Strong Hill Church to these prospective worshipers. Where can they get help?

A congregational worship statement can be a helpful tool for congregations and worship planners, but many churches have not written one. When we ask worship planners about their worship statement, many admit they hadn't ever thought of putting one together. Others admit that although they don't have one, they wish they did. Those who have written such a document have done so carefully and thoughtfully and find it a valuable tool. George Barna, president of Barna Research Group, which specializes in research for Christian churches, says many churches are in trouble because "a majority of adults attending Christian churches have no idea what worship means. Two out of three cannot provide an appropriate definition or description of worship" (Barna, *The Habits of Highly Effective Churches* [Ventura, Calif.: Regal Books, 1999], 84-85). Lutheran writer Marva Dawn warns in *Morning by Morning* (Grand Rapids: Eerdmans, 2001, 3), that we aren't willing to ask enough questions or the right questions about the foundations of what we are doing. "Just as scientists sometimes begin to perform medical procedures before anyone has raised the necessary moral objections, so it seems that many congregations today are switching worship practices without investigating what worship means and how our worship relates to contemporary culture." She goes on to say that the church should be a place of "meaningful talking, attentive listening and profound thinking" (p. 3), the kind that will develop a theology of worship for the church to flourish and grow.

THE VALUE OF A GOOD STATEMENT

The landscape of worship today is marked by so many new ideas, new approaches, and new formats that clarifying our understanding of worship and constructing a congregational worship statement have become urgent matters. Every congregation needs a standard, something written down so that all can refer to it.

We recommend one of two procedures, depending on the polity and institutional ties of your congregation. Some congregations need to start from scratch, either because they are independent, or because they belong to denominations that have no working statements about worship. Other congregations could best start from an approved denominational document. In this case perhaps a congregation could best add a list of implications to the denomination's statement. Even in these cases, however, great value inheres in having a congregation articulate how it applies the denominational document locally.

Each congregation has enough conflicting opinions and preferences to create unsettling confusion unless those who lead provide clear direction. Worship planners confront suggestions and ideas today that they had never anticipated. In addition, we need to reflect our denominational identities, our congregational personalities, and our growing awareness of the richness of ecumenicity. Leadership should develop a carefully formulated statement of the convictions and values that shape worship.

A good worship statement will serve three healthy purposes:

1. *It is a formation tool.* While worship is about God first of all, it also is about the worshipers. While we worship to honor God, we are being formed in the process. Worship is shaped by our theology, and yet we must admit that the way we worship can reshape both our theology and our identity. This influence of worship takes place so subtly that those who lead worship without a carefully written statement may unintentionally be forming a false identity. That is a matter of concern!

2. *It is a measurement tool.* We need a tool to provide an unambiguous set of criteria as the standard for measurement in both planning and evaluating worship services. How do planners know what to plan if the theological principles and the local implications are not identified? And how can they evaluate worship if everyone has a different set of criteria in mind? One worship planner said a worship statement would force the planners to state the essentials and the boundaries of what they believe true worship is. A clear worship statement would help Horizon church know how to respond to those who like to applaud the anthems. And it would guide the planning team at Church of the Valley in evaluating the request for the potluck drama. The biblical virtue of discernment is critical for worship planners, and discernment, the wisdom to determine what is most fitting, can be guided by a defined worship statement.

3. *It is a teaching tool.* Worship leaders today have a large educational task on their hands. Since most worshipers are unable to define worship, part of our task is to teach them what it is that they are engaged in each Sunday. What an excellent tool a worship statement can be! Adult education classes can use it as part of their curriculum. An attractively printed brochure can be made available in the narthex for anyone to read. New-member classes can use it to

---

A Worship Statement Is

1. A formation tool
2. An evaluation tool
3. A teaching tool

---

introduce new members to the worship life of the congregation. Visitors can become better informed. Members like Carl and Mary have a readily available tool to give to their inquiring neighbors who wonder what to expect when they come for worship.

A clear statement of the theology of worship that guides the congregation, and that does so in language and concepts that a layperson can understand, serves these three purposes well. It must therefore include the definition of the biblical understanding of worship, the elements to be included in a worship service, and the characteristics of worship that meaningfully reflect the denominational identity, and that match both the personality of the congregation and its core values.

WHAT SHALL WE INCLUDE?

We have spoken about the importance of such a statement, how it can be used, and what resources should be used. But what should it include? How extensive should it be? What subjects are "musts"? We suggest that five subjects ought to be included.

1. *Our theology of worship.* How we understand God will greatly shape our idea of how to worship. The worship life of a congregation reveals a great deal about our understanding of God. Our perception of God's character and personality will shape how we approach him. Our perception of God's grace and mercy will shape our willingness to be open. Our perception of his compassion will increase our readiness to approach him. Our perception of God's justice will create our penitence. And our perception of God's veracity will increase our trust in his Word and promises.

    We're convinced that the God we worship is a triune God. All three persons of the Trinity must be in focus. In our worship statement we avoided leaving a mistaken impression about the God we worship that might prevail if we neglected any reference to the Son and the Spirit. We didn't want to worship Christ alone with no reference to the Father and the Spirit. Then again, worship focused only on the Spirit and his leading would run the risk of neglecting the other two. And so our worship statement makes clear that we worship a triune God—we give praise and adoration to the Father, whom we have come to know through the mediating work of the Son, prompted by the internal working of the Holy Spirit. Make sure your statement accurately expresses your theology.

2. *The purpose of our worship.* We don't come to worship only to hear about God but also to engage in a personal encounter with him. Anthony Robinson, a minister of the United Church of Christ, puts that issue clearly before us with an old and perhaps apocryphal story about two signs that appeared one day on the sweeping green of the Boston Common. One sign said, "This way to lectures about God." The second said, "This way to God." Robinson adds, "In the civic-faith era—and still in many mainline churches—the crowd (such as it is) is likely to follow the first sign. In the post-Christendom, postmodern era, people are increasingly inclined to the direction of the second sign. They seek God, and they seek access to the sacred." (Robinson, *Transforming Congregational Culture* [Grand Rapids: Eerdmans, 2003], 42). Our purpose of worship must be made clear in our worship statement.

3. *The participants in worship.* For whom are we planning this worship service? What is our view of those who we anticipate will attend? Will they be committed Christians who eagerly desire an encounter with God? Will they be underchurched people who are only nominally Christian and perhaps have not been in church for months? Will they be "seekers" who are not committed but interested in exploring the matter further? Will we assume that they are all adults? Will they be adults of primarily one age bracket? Will youth be present? Will families and children be present? How we answer these questions will shape our task of planning worship in great measure.

4. *The practices of our worship.* Each church needs to make clear how its theology shapes its practice—following the historic liturgy which includes a standard fourfold or fivefold pattern of worship, using the lectionary, celebrating communion monthly, and so on. We must have sound reasons for shaping worship the way we do, and we must be able to articulate those reasons to others if they are to worship with understanding. Christ Lutheran Church, a congregation of the Lutheran Church–Missouri Synod in Sioux Falls, South Dakota, developed a worship statement that includes six major theses or

confessions of what the congregation believes about worship, followed by a paragraph that answers the question, "What does this mean at Christ Lutheran?" The explanations are as important as the theses themselves.

5. *The process for worship planning.* How do we evaluate suggestions? How do we evaluate requests? How do we evaluate and manage change in our worship life? Who is responsible for such matters? If we clearly spell out who is ultimately responsible for our worship life, we will have an identified process for dealing with the kinds of scenarios with which this chapter opened. It will be clear where the discussion about applause should take place, what criteria shape the decision about whether the Thanksgiving potluck drama infomercial is appropriate, and how a group decides whether Derrick may bring his CDs.

If you build your worship statement around these five categories, you will have an excellent start.

Patterns to Follow

No one worship statement will fit all congregations, because churches vary so much in personality, tradition, community, and context. Yet we can learn from others' experiences. Our intention is to provide you with a "visit" to other congregations that have a worship statement. Hearing how others articulate their values and practices can be of great benefit to you in writing a statement for your congregation. Note that some of these documents "define the edges" and state the non-negotiables (for example, "We won't use taped music"). Other documents "articulate the center" and state the key goals and values of worship (for example, "we will enhance the use of psalms"). You will notice that some churches try to balance these two approaches, and we believe it's best to work for a balance.

We provide here a variety of congregational and denominational statements that may help you.

Hillcrest Christian Reformed Church, Hudsonville, Michigan

When we shared ministry in Hillcrest Church, our worship leadership team crafted these statements that expressed the direction of our worship life.

1. *Biblical worship is always God centered.* We are told to come "before him" (Psalm 95:2; 100:2), for "he is our God and we are the people of his pasture" (Psalm 95:7).

2. *Biblical worship is based on the self-revelation of God.* God speaks, and the people are called to respond. God spoke to Moses from the burning bush and on Mount Sinai; to the people of Israel through the message of the prophets; to all through the life, death, resurrection, and ascension of Jesus Christ and through the gift of the Holy Spirit. God continues to address us today through the Word and Holy Spirit.

3. *As God's people respond, they are enriched and blessed.* Asaph was confused about God's ways with the wicked; then he said, "I entered the sanctuary of God; then I understood their final destiny" (Psalm 73:17). Psalm 84 describes the security that worshipers find in the presence of God as greater than the home of a sparrow and the nest of a swallow; and the psalmist exclaims, "Blessed are those who dwell in your house" (v. 4).

4. *Worshipers must approach God with a sense of trust, dependence, awe, and faith.* Historically, many Christian churches have begun their worship services with an expression of humble dependence, using the words of Psalm 124:8, "Our help is in the name of the Lord, the Maker of heaven and earth." Old Testament worshipers were called with these words, "Come, let us bow down in worship, let us kneel before the Lord our Maker; for he is our God and we are the people of his pasture, the flock under his care" (Psalm 95:6-7). Jesus told the Samaritan woman that his "worshipers must worship in spirit and in truth" (John 4:24).

5. *Since worship is a corporate conversation with God, prayer is at the heart of worship.* Prayers may be silent, spoken, or sung; they may be prayers of praise, thanksgiving, confession, petition, or intercession, or cries for help. The words may be read from a printed page, carefully prepared in advance and offered by a worship leader, or spoken extemporaneously from the heart. Much of what we do in worship is prayer.

6. *Music and praise have always played a large role in worship, because God calls his people to sing a new song.* Psalm 96 encourages us to "sing to the Lord a new song," and Revelation 4 and 5 indicate that

a major activity in heaven is singing the new song in praise of God's gracious work in Jesus Christ.

Christ Lutheran Church, Sioux Falls, South Dakota

We've said that music is a large part of worship. Therefore, a worship statement might also include principles and implications about its role. Christ Lutheran Church in Sioux Falls, South Dakota, sought in its worship statement to spell out its understanding of the role of music within the worship life of the church. First, the congregation's conviction was stated positively: "We confess that the purpose of music in the church is to bear the living voice of the Gospel" (Heb. 12:28-29). They immediately followed it with another equally forthright statement: "We deny that music is present for purely aesthetic reasons for the satisfaction of personal tastes of worshipers or worship leaders." They helpfully spelled out the implications of their convictions:

- Appropriate music and art [are] based on the church year and [are] in agreement with Lutheran theology. We seek to incorporate all elements of worship—including hymns, attendant music, and readings—into such a cohesive whole.
- Worship must be thoughtfully prepared and skillfully presented. Assistants must receive careful guidance and direction before serving in [a] congregational service.
- Although music styles change, worthiness and craft, skill and suitability are qualities consistent with our desire to bring God our very best.
- The use of the visual and performing arts, in particular the use of instruments (brass, winds, strings, etc.), is to be encouraged and cultivated.
- The pipe organ remains the best instrument for one person to lead congregational song, because it is a wind instrument which breathes like a singer and produces a variety of sounds.
- We stress that the choir's primary function is the teaching and leading of the congregation's singing of the liturgy and hymns.
- Because our worship is directed to God, the location of the choirs and instrumentalists should encourage congregational singing without attracting the primary focus to the groups.

Christian Reformed Church in North America

The Christian Reformed Church in North American received an extensive study on worship at its 1997 annual denominational gathering. The heart of that report has been published in *Authentic Worship in a Changing Culture* (Grand Rapids: CRC Publications [1-800-333-8300], 1997; used by permission). That report gives eight theses, statements that identify particular gifts that the Reformed tradition has made to Christian worship (76-78).

1. A redemptive-historical perspective on worship (a) that takes seriously the rich communion of relationships in worship—from the relationships between God and his people, to the relationships among God's people (here and now and throughout history—from Abraham to the saints around the throne) and (b) that takes seriously the intimate connection between service and love of God and service and love of neighbor and the need for integrity of these two. Also implicit in this rich redemptive-historical perspective is an understanding of the relationship of church and kingdom that keeps Christian worship always directed out beyond itself into service in every dimension of life in God's world.

2. A fully Trinitarian emphasis in worship that seeks balanced attention to God the Father, God the Son, and God the Holy Spirit.

3. An understanding that preaching is the proclamation of the Word of God that results in a Spirit-charged encounter with God, not mere lecture or instruction. In this connection, it is significant that in Reformed worship the Holy Spirit is traditionally involved not only in the context of the sacraments but also in the context of the reading and preaching of the Word.

4. An emphasis upon doctrinal preaching.

5. Calvin's sacramental theology that emphasizes the real presence of Christ in the sacraments.

6. A particular emphasis upon the acts of worship that arise out of a view of worship as true encounter with God. These include the salutation, the declaration of pardon, the prayer for illumination [before the Word is preached, a prayer is offered to call down the Holy Spirit to open the minds of the congregation to God's Word] and the benediction.

7. A conviction that congregational singing is at the heart of worship music, integrated into every part of worship, and a corresponding caution that congregational singing should not be minimized and/or swallowed up by other forms of worship music.

8. A strong appreciation for the Old Testament in general and for psalm singing in particular as part of public worship. (Much of the Reformed emphasis upon the Psalms and the Old Testament is related to the redemptive-historical theology as set forth above.)

Evangelical Lutheran Church in America

The Evangelical Lutheran Church in America (ELCA) has undertaken an ambitious consultation on renewing worship (*Principles for Worship* [Minneapolis: Augsburg Fortress, 2002]). Taking into consideration the quickened pace of change in the church and beyond, the denomination is in the process of examining the worship life of the church to provide resources for the next generation. As part of this effort, the ELCA has published 124 principles for worship. Subjects of the principles set forth and explained include language, music, preaching, worship space, the use of the means of grace (baptism and Holy Communion), and the relationship between the means of grace and Christian mission. Churches crafting their own worship statements will benefit greatly from studying this material.

Presbyterian Church (U.S.A.)

The Presbyterian Church (U.S.A.) has provided guidelines for worship as set forth in its "Directory for Worship" found in *The Book of Order:*

> Worship [shall] be ordered in terms of five major actions centered in the Word of God—gathering around the Word, proclaiming the Word, responding to the Word, the sealing of the Word [that is, the sacraments are a sign and a seal of the promises of the Word], and bearing and following the Word into the world. Sunday worship usually includes the recitation of the Nicene or Apostles' Creed, or A Brief Statement of Faith. The actual order of worship however is up to the minister and the session [governing board] of an individual congregation. Baptism and Lord's

Supper are the two Sacraments that Presbyterians celebrate. Infants, children, or adults are generally baptized during the worship service by pouring or sprinkling; immersion is rarely used. The Lord's Supper is celebrated regularly, with most congregations celebrating monthly. All baptized Christians are welcome to share in the Lord's Supper, including baptized children.

Authors

Individual authors also have provided valuable background material for writing a congregational worship statement.

Thomas Long, the Bandy professor of preaching at Candler School of Theology, Emory University, and a Presbyterian minister, studied a variety of vital and faithful congregations to learn how "worship can remain true to the trajectory of authentically Christian witness while responding boldly and creatively to the changing currents of our time" (Long, *Beyond the Worship Wars: Building Vital and Faithful Worship* [Alban Institute, 2001], xii). He discovered nine marks that vital and faithful congregations have in common. These nine became the chapters of his book, and might be taken into consideration by churches as they write their worship statements. Such marks can provide a backdrop for your theological statements about your worship life. Long says that vital and faithful congregations:

1. Make room, somewhere in worship, for the experience of mystery.
2. Make planned and concerted efforts to show hospitality to the stranger.
3. Have recovered and made visible the sense of drama inherent in Christian worship.
4. Emphasize congregational music that is both excellent and eclectic in style and genre.
5. Creatively adapt the space and environment of worship.
6. Forge a strong connection between worship and local mission—a connection expressed in every aspect of the worship service.
7. Maintain a relatively stable order of service and a significant repertoire of worship elements and responses that the congregation knows by heart.
8. Move to a joyous festival experience toward the end of the service.
9. Have strong, charismatic pastors as worship leaders.

Harold Best, former dean of the Conservatory of Music at Wheaton College, Wheaton, Illinois, has written *Music through the Eyes of Faith* (HarperSanFrancisco, 1993). If we are to enhance our worship through music, Best says, we must keep in mind the following:

1. Being emotionally moved by music is not the same as being spiritually or morally shaped by it.
2. All true acts of worship are linked to, and supportive of, further acts of worship.
3. Music-as-aid [music-as-aid is not music that brings people to faith, but music that aids the growth of faith] is a different matter for the believer than for the nonbeliever.
4. Being moved by music is secondary to worshiping God.
5. Aesthetic excitement, at whatever level and from whatever source, is as much a part of being human as loving is.

Task-force members assigned the task of writing for their congregation will benefit greatly from reading further and discussing together these insights from Best.

In 2001, in a lecture at St. Olaf College in Northfield, Minnesota, we presented these core values that shape our worship ministries:

1. Worship should be done according to the Scriptures. Scripture gives us instruction for worship in directives, patterns, words, and principles.
2. Our worship should be Trinitarian. That is, we worship a Triune God, Father, Son, and Holy Spirit.
3. The entire Lord's Day should be rich for the Christian. On the first day of the week we gather for worship and celebrate the resurrection of Christ and the outpouring of the Holy Spirit.
4. Worship is a meeting between God and his people, that is, a structured conversation at God's gracious invitation, in which he speaks his word of forgiveness, instruction, and blessing, and God's people respond by celebrating the redemptive work of Christ with acts of confession, adoration, commitment and remembrance.
5. Worship has a clearly defined primary purpose—to give adoration and honor to God. As we fulfill this primary purpose, worshipers

are strengthened and nurtured to live obediently for God in this world.

6. Worship should express humility, make confession, and include an assurance of pardon. All worshipers should come before God penitently as sinful people in need of receiving and being renewed in his grace. God extends his gracious pardon to us from his Word.

7. Worship should be marked by reverence and awe. Revelation 4 and 5 are our models for understanding that the God we worship is holy, majestic, and almighty.

8. Worship must be marked by celebration and joy. God has come in his Son and Spirit, has forgiven and blessed us in his grace, and so we celebrate the victories of his grace.

9. Worship leaders serve a dual role. They stand between God and his people. At times they will speak for God to his people, as in the reading of Scripture and sermon. At other times they will speak for the people to God, as in prayers and intercessions.

10. The proclamation of the Scriptures is the primary means of grace. When God's Word is faithfully proclaimed, faith is nurtured and hearts are strengthened.

11. The sacraments are supplements to the Word of God. Both the Lord's Supper and Baptism are signs and seals of the work of God proclaimed in his Word and should be regularly observed in worship as a means of grace and incorporated meaningfully in the liturgy.

12. Music has emotional power that can be helpful in shaping the worshipers' response. The wedding of text and tune (thought and emotion, or theology and spirit) gives the worshipers effective opportunity to express their praise and prayers to God.

13. The ministry of music is a ministry of the congregation. It is not so much that worshipers need persons and groups to sing to them, but musicians aid them in their own song. The congregation must always remain the primary choir in the congregation.

14. The texts used in worship music must be faithful to the Scriptures and must fit what is occurring in the liturgy. Faithfulness of content and appropriateness in liturgy are both important.

15. Music must be honest. The music should serve the text and not draw attention to itself. The music is a servant to the message of the text.

16. Worship services should include a balance of what is standard and familiar, and what is variable and flexible.

17. We are to be mindful of children and youth and take them seriously in worship. They should be able to participate fully, consciously, and actively in worship at their own developmental level.

18. The gifts of members of the congregation are to be used in worship leadership. Lay members of the body are permitted and encouraged to lead others in worship. It is both a privilege and responsibility to do so.

19. Worship services are to be planned carefully and thoughtfully so that the worshiping community can offer its best to God.

20. The observance of the Christian year provides a rhythm for the worshiping congregation that reenacts annually the major events of God's redemption through Christ and the Spirit.

IMPLICATIONS FOR PRACTICE

As you can see, many have invested great effort in writing their statements about worship. You'll also notice variety in the matters addressed and in how comprehensive each statement is. Observing the efforts of others can guide us all in writing our own.

All principles have implications. So, in addition to spelling out the principles that shape our thinking about worship, these statements are most useful when they include guidelines for putting the principles into practice. Formulate the guidelines carefully, preferably through a group process within the worship committee or planning team, because some statements of practice are likely to stir up debate. In fact, you will discover that most discussions in the worship committee or among worship planners focus on the implications of principles. Some of the stories at the opening of this chapter illustrate the issues of practice confronting us and requiring resolution.

In our ministries in Hudsonville, Michigan, we spelled out some of the implications of our principles in this manner:

1. Since those who are familiar with the life of our congregation are best able to lead us in worship, leaders should generally be members of this congregation. Whenever others are included, there must be careful integration and coordination.

2. The role of all worship leaders, whether individuals or groups, shall not be to worship for others but to lead others to worship more meaningfully.

3. It is appropriate for lay members of all ages to lead the whole community in worshiping. All who lead in worship must be prepared well, integrated into the liturgy carefully, and competent to lead according to their developmental level.

4. Music is the offering and response by the worshipers in a given situation. It evokes a spontaneous response to a specific moment in worship and, therefore, it should be live, not prerecorded. Those requiring amplified sound should use the church's sound system.

5. The use of appropriate visual aids in the sanctuary is encouraged for the purpose of creating a worshipful atmosphere and directing the hearts and minds of the worshipers.

6. The use of drama is appropriate, not as a production or performance, but as a helpful aid to the corporate meeting between God and his people.

7. The primary responsibility for planning the worship services shall be that of the senior pastor and the director of music in consultation with the worship committee and the elders. All other worship leaders shall serve under their direction.

8. All those who serve in worship service support capacities (such as video and sound technicians, custodians, ushers, etc.) shall carry out their tasks carefully and responsibly to aid in meaningful worship.

The Neland Avenue Christian Reformed Church of Grand Rapids, Michigan, addressed the matter of music in spelling out the implications of their worship statement.

1. The music should represent the best of the past and present from ethnic traditions that closely reflect the church's membership, both local and universal.

2. The music should be an integral part of congregational worship and constitute an onward movement of the worship experience.

3. The music should direct the worshiper to the Creator more than to the creature, to worship more than to entertainment.

4. The music should aid congregational participation and unity. Words of choir or solo selections should normally be printed in the bulletin when legally possible.

Writing the Worship Statement

Writing a worship statement is no small task. Perhaps that's why so many congregations don't yet have one, though they realize that a statement would be helpful. To write such a statement hurriedly or without careful formulation could be worse than not having one at all. Take your time and plan to spend at least six months on the project.

The preaching pastor should serve as the key person in this process. Writing a worship statement can hardly be done without the pastor's participation. The initial suggestion may come from a congregational member, but the pastor, at the very least, should provide the primary encouragement to a small group to begin the effort. The group should engage in the research and writing, however, so that the statement is not only the pastor's work. These people might include members from the worship committee, particularly the presiding officer, and from the worship planning team. As they write, they will surely want to invite evaluations and suggestions from others who are knowledgeable in worship matters. Don't be surprised that this statement goes through multiple drafts!

The entire worship committee and the ruling body of the church should approve the statement in its final form. In that way it becomes an official statement of the congregation about its life of worship.

No one can or should adopt such an important document without consulting other resources. First, be sure the process involves a careful study of Scripture and its teachings about worship. Scripture contains direct instructions about worship, principles to guide us in worship, and patterns of worship to follow. We encourage you to include a study of your own congregation's history and to maintain a lively conversation with the tradition that has shaped you. That includes consulting the creeds and confessions of your denomination and statements from official assemblies, but also researching the minutes of past meetings of your congregation and its ruling board. You can also draw on your local identity as a congregation. What factors have shaped you as a community? What is the unique personality of your congregation and how does it influence your worship life? What in your history has shaped your identity?

Avoid excessively technical theological terms to ensure that the entire statement is accessible to the average member of the congregation.

Writing a worship statement may include the following steps:

1. Plan a group discussion with worship planners, the worship committee, and staff members to identify the current needs and concerns of your congregation that need to be addressed in a worship statement. Ask such questions as: What is the overall vitality of our worship life? How well does our congregation understand what worship is? What uncertainties about worship must we aim to clarify? What are the tension points in our worship life? What is the best method of communicating with our congregation on these matters?

2. Clearly identify who will be responsible for taking the lead in writing this statement. Who will be part of the group that researches and writes? Who will be drawn in to evaluate and review it for further modification? Who will need to give final approval?

3. Study the Scriptures on the matter of worship. Examine the patterns of worship in the Tabernacle, the Temple, and the New Testament church. Explore the variety and use of the Psalms. Research the meaning of the words used in the Bible such as praise, adoration, confession, serve, thanks, fear, awe, bow, prostrate. Study the scene of worship in Revelation 4 and 5 and in other passages.

4. Consult the resources that your theological and denominational tradition provide. Creeds, confessions, denominational statements, and studies concerning worship and policy are helpful.

5. Research the documents and minutes of your congregation. What is available to review and build on?

6. Read materials written by authors who examine the themes of worship in Scripture. Here are some of the most recent publications that we suggest:

   • Dawn, Marva. *A Royal "Waste" of Time: The Splendor of Worshiping God and Being Church for the World.* Grand Rapids: Eerdmans, 1999.

The Process of Writing a Worship Statement

1. A group discussion to identify our needs
2. Appointment of those responsible for writing
3. A group study of the Scriptures on worship
4. Consultation of denominational resources
5. Research of local documents and minutes
6. A study of other authors on the subject
7. A review of worship statements from other congregations
8. Formulation of the worship statement

- Mitman, Russell. *Worship in the Shape of Scripture.* Cleveland: Pilgrim Press, 2001.
- Old, Hughes Oliphant. *Worship Reformed according to Scripture.* Louisville: Westminster John Knox, 2002.
- Peterson, David. *Engaging With God: A Biblical Theology of Worship.* Downers Grove, Ill.: InterVarsity Press, 1992.
- Plantinga, Cornelius Jr., and Sue A. Rozeboom. *Discerning the Spirits: A Guide to Thinking about Christian Worship Today.* Grand Rapids: Eerdmans, 2003.
- Witvliet, John D. *Worship Seeking Understanding: Windows into Christian Practice.* Grand Rapids: Baker Academic, 2003.

7. Review others' worship statements. At the end of this chapter a variety of sample formulations is included for you to consider as you write your own. You will notice that while each of these samples reflects the community of faith for which it was written, they all aim to accomplish the same thing. No church can merely adopt another church's statement, because each has its own personality and culture. Yet you will be able to review these with great profit. As you read them, identify the purpose that each church had in mind, the major themes addressed, the method of addressing these themes, and the "readability" of each one.

8. Write the statement! When it's time to put thoughts into writing, select one person as the primary drafter to formulate the thoughts of the group. Assume that the document will go through several drafts as the group edits it.

Writing the statement can be an intensive and time-consuming task but one that is worth the effort and time it requires. A congregation will be well served by a carefully written worship statement.

Sample Statements

We provide a variety of sample worship statements because we believe that reflection and discussion on these will enrich your own. Please note that these are all actual statements, though different in format, that guide congregations in their worship. They represent various denominations, worship styles, and communities.

Sample 1
Neland Avenue Christian Reformed Church,
Grand Rapids, Michigan

1. *Worship at Neland Church must be inclusive as well as Reformed.* By "inclusive," it is established that we are not trying simply to assimilate people of other cultures into our own. Rather, we seek to discover, affirm, and utilize the riches and strengths of the worship traditions of those to whom and with whom we are ministering. By "inclusive," it is also established that worship planners and leaders will be vigilant in identifying and removing unnecessary barriers that unwittingly exclude those who do not share a traditional Christian Reformed background.

   By "Reformed," it is affirmed that Neland Church has a particular identity, historically and theologically, in the Christian church, and that the goal of Neland Church in worship is to work out of, not to forget or obliterate, that identity. The call to inclusivity is not understood as a call to abandon those things that make us distinctive, historically and/or theologically, or to reduce worship to the lowest common denominator of several different ethnic backgrounds. The call to inclusivity is a call to each church (e.g., Pentecostal churches, Baptist churches, Lutheran churches, and Christian Reformed churches), with its own particular history and identity, to be inclusive in worship.

2. *Worship at Neland Church must be warm and personal as well as ordered and dignified.* By its very definition, worship is deeply personal and deeply social. Christ-centered and Spirit-empowered worship will communicate and embody the love of Christ and the love of Christ's people for one another. Elements of worship like "mutual greetings" are specific occasions for people to affirm that they are one with one another in the body of Christ. Every effort must be made to plan and carry out worship in such a way that the personal and social reality of our life in Christ is experienced.

Regarding "ordered" worship, it is important that "warm and personal" not be equated with "informal, spontaneous, or unplanned." "Warmth" and "order" are not mutually contradictory marks of worship. The theological heart of Reformed worship is worship as dialogue with God. Generally speaking, worship services should be carefully planned and well ordered to capture, celebrate and carry out that dialogue.

Regarding "dignified" worship, it is important that "warm and personal" not be construed in such a way that the awe and dignity of worship is undercut. Worship reflects both God's immanence and his transcendence: he is at once very close and personal, and very great and awesome. Worship must communicate warmth and awe, the closeness and the grandeur of God. In this regard, Neland Church must be aware of the perils of ministering in a narcissistic culture in which even Christian worship can become self absorbed, just one more mechanism for self-fulfillment. Worship must bring those who have come to worship beyond themselves to God.

3. *Worship at Neland Church must be flexible and varied as well as predictable and stable.* Within the broad purposes of worship, each worship service is unique. It takes place on a particular Sunday, in a particular congregation, led by a particular preacher who has particular purposes in mind for this worship service in general and sermon in particular. Jesus' teaching that the new wine of the gospel requires new wineskins is, among other things, a call for worship to be dynamic, flexible, and varied according to the needs and purposes of a particular worship service.

At the same time, there must be predictability and stability in worship, for several reasons:

a. People have a legitimate need and desire for pattern and norm in worship. Every area of life is characterized by a need for pattern, ritual, and routine. Worship leaders must recognize the same need in worship.

b. In the very nature of the Christian faith as a historical faith, worship must communicate to those present that they belong to something bigger than themselves, bigger than last week.

c. In a world where things are changing at a rate beyond our comprehension, worship must offer to those present a participation in something that has endured and will endure through the ups and downs of not just this particular week, but of the generations.

Sample 2
First Presbyterian Church, Wheaton, Illinois

At this congregation a group of staff members, under the guidance of the pastor, collaboratively formulated this expression of the church's worship theology. These guidelines were used for instruction and setting the vision of the church in worship. Notice how this "Worship Vision Statement" begins with a quotation from the Directory for Worship of the Presbyterian Church (U.S.A.).

Christian worship joyfully ascribes all praise and honor, glory and power to the triune God. In worship the people of God acknowledge God as present in the world and in their lives. As they respond to God's claim and redemptive action in Jesus Christ, believers are transformed and renewed. In worship the faithful offer themselves to God and are equipped for God's service in the world.

1. *Our worship is Presbyterian.* We have an identity. Our worship identifies with a particular history that gives meaning to our faith. Therefore, the basic patterns and forms and rhythms of our worship are givens. The Word, for example, is and will continue to be central to our worship, both in preaching and in the sacraments.

2. *Our worship is participatory.* When we worship, we are encouraged to be actively involved; we are called to be more than passive observers of what happens "up front." We think of our order of worship as a kind of script or drama in which we all play important parts, prompted and led by our worship leaders.

3. *Our worship is vital, dynamic, and exuberant.* In worship we give expression to our faith in different ways and with different gifts. Our spirit is evident in all we do; the movement of the Spirit in our worship is something we pray for and hope to experience regularly.

4. *Our worship is inclusive of all ages.* The youngest children are no less important to our worship than our oldest adults. We seek to include children by planning worship that has movement, color, drama, freshness, and a varied pace. We find ways to include our youth in ways they find significant and meaningful. Families are encouraged to worship together and to make Sunday morning an important family time. Singles are encouraged to feel a part of the larger church family. Older adults delight in the presence of children as evidence that the faith is being passed on to a new generation.

5. *Our worship is always provisional.* We are feeling our way in a changing world, seeking ways to worship that are fitting for our church and faithful to God. We are encouraged to use our gifts of creativity and imagination, knowing that not all attempts will be successful or long lasting. Our worship will be perfect only in the glorious celebration of the life to come.

6. *Our worship is a time of grace.* From beginning to end, in everything we do, we strive in our worship to give expression to the grace we have felt in Jesus Christ. This means we are welcoming and hospitable to those who visit with us. This means our tone in worship is affirming and celebrating, not judging and shaming. This means we are always finding ways to make visible and real the unconditional love and acceptance of Jesus Christ.

7. *Our worship provides an opportunity for a life-changing encounter with Jesus Christ.* Our worship is most successful when worshipers sense the presence and power of Jesus Christ and are changed in significant and dramatic ways because of it. The best way we know of to "do evangelism" is to lead people into the presence of Jesus Christ where they can be changed by him.

Sample 3
Christ Lutheran Church, Sioux Falls, South Dakota

Christ Lutheran Church has titled its worship statement "Worship in our Congregation: The Triune God serves us in the Divine Service with His Word and sacraments." This worship statement is built around six theses, each of which includes a statement and a counterstatement. Each of the six begins with "we confess . . ." and then "we deny . . ." follows.

Thesis 1—We confess that worship *(Gottesdienst)* is our triune God's service to us, and our faithful responses always direct us back to God from whom all blessings flow. We deny that worship is primarily a human activity, which is constituted by contrived efforts at emotion-centered adoration and praise (Matt. 20:28; Luke 22:24-27; Acts 1:1, 2).

Thesis 2—We confess that worship flows from the Gospel. At the heart and center of all worship is Jesus Christ and His atoning sacrifice for sin. In worship, the living and saving Lord comes to give us life. We deny that worship is based on the Law, namely, that our feelings or gifts supplement the work of Christ (Luke 24:25-35).

Thesis 3—We confess that in the liturgy God's Word and sacraments are proclaimed and administered. Through these means, God dispenses forgiveness, life, and salvation (John 4:21-24; 1 Cor. 2:6-16). We deny that the liturgy is a mere form to produce the desired responses in worshipers.

Thesis 4—We confess that the purpose of music in the church is to bear the living voice of the Gospel (Heb. 12:28-29). We deny that music is present for purely aesthetic reasons or for the satisfaction of personal tastes of worshipers or worship leaders.

Thesis 5—We confess that worship is catholic (that is, universal). The gathering of God's people around Word and Sacrament reaches across cultural and social barriers to transcend both time and space. We deny that worship is defined by the tastes and preferences of an individual or group of worshipers.

Thesis 6—We confess that the environment of worship should be theologically sound, aesthetically pleasing, and spiritually edifying. We deny that art and architecture are neutral factors in a setting for worship (1 Cor. 10:23-31).

Sample 4
Church of the Servant, Christian Reformed,
Grand Rapids, Michigan

This congregation had its beginning in the 1960s and has thought-fully formulated a worship statement that reflects both its basic theology and the personality of the congregation.

Worship—becoming a prism of God's light in liturgy and life. We will proclaim the good news of the Lord Jesus Christ with worship that is catholic, celebrative, and participatory, so that the faithful will be nourished and so that the seeker may encounter in worship the living Lord.

Catholic . . . Church of the Servant liturgies draw upon a wide range of Christian sources and traditions. All of our liturgies follow the same basic structure, a structure inspired by the example of the early church and used today in churches of many different denominations.

This structure has two main focal points: Word and Sacrament. In Scripture and sermon we hear God speaking to us; in the sacraments we experience the assurance that the promises of the gospel are "for real," and we become united more closely to Christ and to one another. The Lord's Supper, therefore, forms a regular part of our weekly worship. When baptism is not administered as part of the service, the baptismal font is often carried forward in procession at an appropriate point in the liturgy as a sign of our redemption and new life in Christ.

Celebrative . . . Our worship celebrates the mighty acts of God in history and the good news of God's grace in our lives. The various seasons of the church year, such as Advent, Lent, Easter, and Pentecost, draw us into active remembrance of decisive events in the life of Christ and the building of God's kingdom. In the sacraments we receive and respond to Christ's self-giving with joy and gratitude.

Although our liturgies are carefully structured, we do not want them to be stiff and formal. There is always room for spontaneity—laughter, tears, clapping, even dancing. Freedom within structure is one of the hallmarks of our worship.

Participatory... At Church of the Servant, worship is not a spectator activity; everyone is invited to become an active participant. Our liturgies include many sections in which we are all asked to speak or sing. We share the peace of Christ with our neighbors. We leave our seats to present our offerings. We walk forward, form circles, and minister the body and blood of Christ to each other at communion. Even younger children have their parts to play. They frequently come forward to witness baptism first hand, and they process out for "Children's Worship" during a part of the service.

Opportunities for worship leadership abound. Members of the congregation regularly read Scripture, lead in prayer, and offer testimonies. Others provide musical leadership as cantors or instrumentalists. Still others give form to faith by means of liturgical dance and art.

For more hands-on involvement in Church of the Servant worship programs, consider joining the Worship Committee, Music Committee, Art Committee, or Liturgical Dance Committee.

> *You will notice both similarities and differences in these sample statements. Each church situation is different, yet the principles remain much the same. By carefully studying what others have written, you can better determine how to write your own statement. Though the task of formulating and writing the statement may be an arduous one, it is worth every effort you expend on it.*

Making It Useful

One of the big concerns all worship leaders have about a worship statement is that writing it could become a wasted effort. They fear that it will become nothing more than one more document lost in a pile of paper. In our correspondence with worship leaders across North America we have often heard this concern expressed. One said, "It has been some time since I've seen it lying around on the information table, but perhaps new members are getting copies of it." Another said, "Right now its role is minimal. The document is seven years old and not much attention is paid to it on a regular basis." Several admitted they don't refer to the document often. To be sure, these are major concerns. No one wants to take on a difficult task with no assurance that the document will serve a lasting and useful role. Yet, there is much potential for good in spelling out the principles that guide worship and its planning process.

The three healthy purposes of the worship statement that we listed earlier in this chapter can guide the use of it. Use the statement as a formation tool that shapes the character and identity of a congregation at worship. Use it as an evaluation tool that sets criteria for measurement in both the planning and the evaluation of worship. And use it as a teaching tool both for congregational members and visitors.

Remembering these purposes, we suggest that your worship statement function in this way:

1. The worship committee regularly studies this document, at least annually, in the course of its work. Perhaps its first session of a new season, or when new committee members join, is an ideal time.
2. Worship planners should review this document at least semi-annually to keep their theology of worship accurately in focus.
3. Each church board member should each have a copy of this document, and it should be reviewed whenever new members join the board. It then becomes instructional for new members and a healthy review for others.
4. The worship statement should be printed and placed prominently in a literature rack where entering worshipers will notice it.

Worship Statement Uses

1. Study within the worship committee
2. Study by worship planners
3. Orientation with new church board members
4. Printed brochure for the literature rack
5. Printed brochure in the pew racks
6. Assistance for worship visitors
7. Basis for instruction in adult education classes
8. Basis for instruction with youth education
9. Basis for instruction in new-member classes
10. Criteria for worship evaluation
11. Sermon topic

---

5. The worship statement, or a summary of it, should be printed in an attractive, readable, and compact brochure and made available in each pew. Worshipers will easily pick up and browse through something right in their line of sight in the pew racks.
6. The brochure is given to all worship visitors to assist them in understanding the church and its worship.
7. The worship statement becomes the focus in the church's adult education or Sunday school classes. Perhaps two or three sessions could be offered periodically.
8. The worship statement becomes subject material for instruction in the youth education classes of the church, for both middle-school and high-school youth. Each class should be exposed to the principles of worship at least once a year.
9. The worship statement is a subject of study and discussion in the church's new-member classes. Obviously, those preparing for full membership will need to deepen their thinking about their worship life.
10. The worship statement provides the criteria for worship evaluation by the planners and committee. If evaluations are to be based on helpful criteria, then evaluation questions and forms should be shaped by this worship statement.
11. The pastor frequently refers to the worship statement in sermons, and preaches annually on the biblical meaning of Christian worship, using this document as a teaching tool.

Just Think . . .

Imagine a congregation that has produced a thoughtful, well-written worship statement. A group of leaders has worked with the pastor to formulate the shape of Christian worship in this congregation. Members of the congregation understand their identity and what worship is. They have the assurance that worship is planned according to a theology that has been thought through, not merely following a whim or trend. The worship committee members are all aware of the principles that shape their leadership. Worship planners better understand what is expected of them, and their work is richer because they understand its purpose. And when it comes time to evaluate worship, the criteria are clear. Here is a church with a highly useful tool.

Imagine if Susan and others had such a statement to guide them in evaluating the applause at Horizon Church. And imagine how much more easily the discussion would have gone in the worship planning meeting at Church of the Valley when the group considered the request to include the "Potluck Drama." And what if Hope Church worship planners had had this document to guide them in responding to Derrick's request to sing with a prerecorded accompaniment? And what if Carl and Mary had been able to put a clear, understandable, and attractive brochure in the hands of the McFarleys?

Clear worship principles will make good worship work even better.

CHAPTER 4

PLANNING THE WORSHIP CALENDAR

Betsy is a choir director and needs to plan. She considers it important that she receive adequate worship information far enough ahead of time that she can make her selections carefully. She loves to spend time browsing through the church's music files to study what is available and consistent with various themes and actions in worship. She has also developed a file of possible music selections that are either newly published or just great music not in the church's music library. If she needs to order music, she always estimates that the shipment will take at least two weeks to arrive, and that the choir will need at least three rehearsals to learn it. She considers it important for the sake of her ministry that the other worship planners sketch out the season early enough to give her time to do this advance work. She knows all participants need to be well prepared to lead the congregation in worship with music that is fitting to a particular service.

Marie and Jack have been co-pastors at Wellspring Church for seven years now. They have always worked together compatibly, sharing the duties of ministry equally, and investing great energy in their worship planning. They thrive on being creative, and the congregation responds to their planning. But this year was different. Their planning sessions were getting shorter and shorter. Neither of them seemed able to summon the creative energy they previously had. The worship committee noticed this and gently engaged them in a discussion about what was happening. After some awkward discussion, Marie finally put her finger on it. "We're just burned out," she blurted. "We've done this for so long we don't have ideas anymore!" It was quite an evening for the committee, but the members finally worked through the pain and came to a consensus. If Jack and Marie could focus on the Christian year and see it as a reenactment of the gospel of Christ, they wouldn't feel the burden of "creating each season" of worship.

Stacey is a gifted artist who loves to provide artwork for the worship space at the church. She is also committed to helping others develop their artistic talent. With the blessing and encouragement of the church, she began an "Artist Apprentice Ministry." She was delighted when eight people expressed interest in joining this small group. She was particularly pleased that the eight were of various ages. It was exciting to her to think of helping these eight develop their artistic abilities and use them in the worship ministry of the church. In her mind she could see colorful banners hanging in front and new pottery on the communion table, and her apprentices fulfilled and legitimately satisfied with their work. But she knew it would take months for young artists to complete their work. She called the pastor to ask about the worship themes for the coming season so they could coordinate their efforts. A long silence followed; then the pastor said: "We have no idea yet . . ."

We all live by calendars. At the turn of the year we remove old ones and post new ones. We discard an appointment book and buy a new one. Schools work with a calendar. So do businesses. The church's educational program works by a calendar. And so must the worship life of the church. It's not sufficient to say that worship will take place every week all year. We must envision what that worship will include. In other words, the calendar must be filled with the ideas, themes, events, and emphases that will shape our worship life. In this chapter we'll talk about the importance of setting a long-term direction for worship through the year. Worship calendars must not only reveal that worship services will take place, but must also sketch the seasons and themes at least in broad strokes. For instance, in September, we should be able to say what the worship themes for February will be. Will Lent be observed? How? These are questions that cannot be answered satisfactorily a few weeks before services. They are more easily addressed and answered when the calendar for the entire year is laid out.

In some congregations the observance of the Christian year is an un-questioned practice. In such instances, planning is easier, but the question becomes what emphasis to provide in each season.

When we speak of a worship calendar, we are talking about a 12-month road map that will identify the intent and focus of worship along the way. Later in this chapter, we will talk about the types of calendars that might be followed. Whatever the calendar, however, it will include (1) the seasons to be observed, (2) special events, and (3) in some congregations, the sched-uled times for celebration of the sacraments and major series of sermons. Obviously, planning in detail can not be done 12 months ahead. The fur-ther ahead we look in that 12-month plan, the more general the projections will be. It is wise to remember, however, that travelers need to know at the beginning of the journey what route they will take. The same is true for worship travelers.

GREAT BENEFITS

To be sure, it takes work to chart out the worship calendar for 12 months. Some, because of denominational resources or personality traits and work styles, will find it much easier than others to plan. In our ministries we have always discovered great benefits in planning a worship calendar. In talking to other worship planners, we've learned that they experience many of the same benefits. Perhaps if we identify some of those benefits, people who find it difficult to plan will be encouraged to develop this healthy habit.

1. *Planning a worship calendar will improve the quality of worship.* This is a bold statement, but those who chart out an entire season of worship will be able to plan more creatively, resulting in better quality. A colleague wrote that this approach gives time for ideas to take shape and gives the members of the planning team a chance to mull over the service themes for weeks and months. Using a planning calendar enables a team to contribute efforts of higher quality.

2. *A worship calendar gives a greater sense of direction.* When we have an overview of the entire year, we will be better prepared to plan each month and week. We can work with the parts when we see the whole. It is particularly rewarding to look over an entire season and see a clear direction. A pastor told us he experiences a thrill when he

sees both the focus and diversity of the seasons—the waiting and hope of Advent give way to the penitence and reflection of Lent, which flow into the joy and celebration of Eastertide and the growth of the Pentecost season. Our songs and our prayers take on a new richness when we see the full sweep of God's work.

3. *A worship calendar makes possible adequate preparation time for all leaders.* Not only preachers, but also musicians and artists need lead time for their planning. If we expect high-quality efforts from others, they need both information and sufficient lead time to do the necessary research, purchases, and preparation of materials and people. We extend a greater courtesy to them when we sketch a worship calendar. Those who plan on a short deadline need to acknowledge that they put their colleagues in planning at a severe disadvantage. In this chapter's opening illustrations, we saw that Betsy needed time to make her selections and prepare her choir and that Stacey's apprentices needed time to design and construct their banners and pottery.

4. *All are able to put more thought and creativity into worship planning.* Short notice and short-range planning lead to missed opportunities, but those who see a whole year ahead are able to give more careful thought to each season, to collect ideas and information, and to discover more resources. One worship planner admitted that some of his most creative thoughts come while driving or taking a shower. So when ideas come, he can take note to file them away for future use. This approach results in a worship life for the church that reflects a greater contribution from each planner and leader. One planning team, while thinking ahead to Advent, decided that the Nicene Creed should be used each week during the gathering time. They spent a few months reflecting on this decision and the best way to accomplish it. When the season arrived, they found that the use of the creed had a cumulative effect. The pastor wrote, "If our planning committee hadn't taken time to think through this use of the creed and what it would do for us, I doubt this element of worship would have had nearly the effect it did."

5. *Greater variety is possible.* The overview of the year allows the worship planners to give a different emphasis to each season, eliminating "sameness" and adding variety. One pastor found that a greater

The Benefits of Seasonal Planning

1. Improvement in quality
2. A greater sense of direction
3. Preparation time for leaders
4. Greater thought and creativity
5. Greater variety
6. Better balance
7. The movement of the Holy Spirit
8. Protection against afterthoughts
9. Greater personal enrichment
10. Avoidance of panic

variety of people can be involved in leadership, from visual artists to instrumentalists. They also found that a greater variety of worship experiences could be offered to worshipers. Those who needed quiet and meditation could find it in Advent and Lent, and those who delighted in joyful celebration found that in other seasons.

6. *Better balance can be achieved.* Worship planners risk falling into a pattern of their own liking or repeating their favorite themes too often. The nurture of a congregation requires an overall balance— in Scripture and preaching, in the tone and themes of worship. All parts of the story of salvation must be in focus at one time or another. Charting out an entire year will make such balance attainable. One pastor wrote that seasonal planning gives her the opportunity to see if she and the congregation are receiving a full representation of all the major parts of Scripture (Epistles, Psalms, Gospels, Prophets, etc.) and whether the whole range of God's drama of redemption is being presented.

7. *The Holy Spirit has room to move.* Some believe that the Spirit works best spontaneously and fear that careful planning will inhibit the work of the Spirit. We believe that the Spirit also does his work while moving through the efforts of the team over an extended period. A worship planner from Canada said his team believes that the Spirit, who desires exciting and vibrant worship, needs time to move through the entire team. The Spirit moves through the team in this planning process, so when planning reaches its final stages, they believe they are offering the Spirit's work back to him. Another

colleague recalls how the unexpected terrorist attacks of September 11, 2001, illustrated that the Holy Spirit had directed them in their planning. The previous spring the pastor had been led to schedule a sermon on Job 1 and 2 for what turned out to be the Sunday following the attacks.

8. *We are protected against afterthoughts.* Every worship leader tardily thinks of wonderful ideas and wishes that they had come to mind earlier. Such ideas usually come after the worship service in question—often late Sunday night! Advance work on a calendar gives opportunity for each season to incubate and gel, thereby minimizing the risk of glaring omissions. Planning teams often have three-ring binders or computer files with designated sections for all the coming seasons. As ideas come, they can be recorded for future consideration. They find advance work has minimized the risk of being haunted by afterthoughts.

9. *Worship planners are personally enriched.* When we walk through an entire worship year, we sense the breadth of the drama of God's work and the flow of a congregation's seasonal engagements with God. Anticipation, planning, leading, and reflecting are satisfying experiences for worship leaders. One worship leader testified to the richness of the revolving calendar, which revisits the reenactment of God's great acts in Christ. Another planner said, "It was wonderful to see how these elements tied together different styles and services throughout the seasons." A worship coordinator said she is careful to study all the Scripture passages for the day and to reflect on them before she selects songs. She finds that a whole season of such study deeply enriches her own life. "Planning itself becomes worship," she said.

10. *Worship planners avoid a sense of panic.* We've never liked the sense of panic that can sweep over us when we sense that deadlines are approaching rapidly and we aren't adequately prepared. Such panic destroys the spirit of our work and decreases our ability to think clearly. We find that panic eats away at creativity, as well as frays the relationships among those who work together. An organist said he is constantly frustrated with the worship coordinator's tardiness because he must select and prepare his music under a harsh deadline. But another musician enjoys her planning because she has been given

each of the dates for Holy Communion and can do extra preparation thoughtfully.

We're convinced that setting an annual worship calendar is the direction to take. Planning worship only month by month or week by week will likely create an undernourished congregation and a drained worship planning team.

A REALITY CHECK

Even, however, as we spell out the benefits that we believe seasonal planning offers, we're realistic enough to know that it won't always go so easily.

Marva Dawn, who frequently writes on worship, encourages us always to remember that worship is for God (Dawn, *How Shall We Worship?* [Wheaton, Ill,: Tyndale House, 2003], 19). So we must check ourselves regularly to ensure that our focus is not on humans and what they want, but on God and what he desires and deserves. Dawn warns us that the culture of narcissism in the early 21st century tempts us to excessive concern about "marketing" our worship. She also warns of the danger of asking the wrong questions about worship, especially when we are confronted with declining church attendance and decreasing denominational membership. Instead of asking how we can best praise and glorify God, we begin to ask, "[W]hat can we do to attract the unbeliever?" (22). This tendency to become utilitarian can easily lead us away from what is primary. Having the whole season of worship in mind can help us avoid such traps.

In another of her books, Dawn points out two other problems than can sidetrack us. Because many have been more concerned with what pleases people than with what pleases God, they have "given in to the consumer's wishes to be merely entertained, lazy, mindless, just like the world, successful or rebellious against all that the Church has been" (*A Royal "Waste" of Time* [Grand Rapids: Eerdmans, 1999], 297). Consequently, worship planners lose their interest and ability to work hard and study well. Maybe you are finding accommodation to culture among those with whom you work. Then we tend to ask the wrong questions, focusing on what people want as opposed to what is appropriate for the worship of God. Seasonal planners need to pay special attention to these traps to keep the entire season on course.

When we plan worship for a whole year, we will face challenges to overcome and irritants we must live with. When people begin planning

Obstacles to Seasonal Planning

1. The wrong focus in worship
2. The wrong questions
3. An unwillingness to work hard
4. Contrasting work styles
5. Control by chaos
6. Time pressures
7. Contingencies and emergencies

collaboratively, different work styles show up, sometimes creating stress. Some folk are better able to anticipate and conceptualize events than others. Some are simply more motivated than others to look ahead. In such instances, the planning process bogs down and stress builds. Worship planning today requires much more collaboration than a generation ago. It is important that all those who serve together are committed to a long-range seasonal planning process, that they encourage each other in learning how to plan, and that they are able mutually to address stress points candidly.

A more severe challenge seasonal planners may face is the chaos created by unclear expectations. This turmoil occurs when roles are not clearly defined or when some refuse to plan. Later we will make the case that the pastor is usually the "first planner" if a season is to be planned well, but others must soon step into the process. Chaos can result if anyone fails to carry out agreed-upon planning tasks. Some who study systems of human behavior speak of the control that some people exert through chaos. One person can virtually control the entire seasonal planning process through the upheaval caused by failure to cooperate.

Of course, we all encounter the difficulty of full calendars and the time pressures of everyday work. Seasonal worship planning takes intentional time management. It can't be done in a few quick hours or on the run. We find it requires a large block of time away from distractions, and it is usually difficult to find that kind of time. Pastors find it hard because their ministries are already filled with a myriad of other tasks. Other staff members have the same problem. Volunteer planners also have full calendars. In describing the process later in the chapter, we recommend that a block of time—a week of study leave or retreat—be set aside for this purpose. It's virtually impossible to establish a calendar in any other way.

A seasonal calendar can be upset by unexpected circumstances in the community. No worship planner can anticipate what will happen in a given season, and sometimes events will disrupt the planned worship calendar. Occasionally a planning team will have only a few days to modify the planned liturgy. Or an emergency may arise that requires the pastor to assume responsibility for reshaping the liturgy. So a planning calendar must leave room for the unexpected. Don't make the calendar too inflexible. Be ready to alter well-laid plans as pastorally necessary.

We must be realistic about the challenges to seasonal planning. But by identifying and remaining aware of them, we can cope. For the sake of vital worship it is important that we do.

KEY PEOPLE

Obviously, planning doesn't begin with paper or a calendar. It begins with people. People determine whether planning happens. And people determine its quality. So who are the people that make this strategy work?

The pastor usually takes the lead in the planning process. Where there are multiple pastors, their roles will determine who serves in this capacity. One may be the primary minister of preaching. Or if there are two (or more) pastors who share the preaching responsibilities equally, they will serve together on the planning team. In a smaller church with a sole pastor, it is obvious where the process begins.

This arrangement is natural and reasonable. The pastor is usually perceived as the "keeper of worship," and the congregation expects that its pastor will play the primary role in worship planning. Being theologically trained, the pastor customarily takes the lead in understanding the seasons of the church year. Most pastors have been trained to understand that worship should reflect the various movements of God throughout the Christian year. The pastor determines the preaching diet of the congregation; much of the other planning should wait until preaching plans are known. The preacher presents the Word of God, and the Word of God must shape our worship more than any other factor. In some congregations where other staff persons are responsible for the work of preaching, the pastor may be joined by another pastor or a worship coordinator so that they set out such a calendar collaboratively, but even then the primary preaching pastor takes the key initiating role.

Pastors need to understand how influential their actions are when they set out their plans for another year, and they should plan prayerfully and thoughtfully. Their selections will influence how well worship and preaching are integrated, how well the whole range of Christian truth is preached, and how carefully pastoral needs are addressed.

Two major ingredients must shape planning—the seasons of the Christian year and the year's preaching plan. In some traditions, the Christian year and the lectionary will in turn be the primary shapers of the preaching plans. We encourage the observance of the Christian year. The journey from Advent through Lent, Eastertide, and Pentecost gives an excellent rhythm to the worshiping congregation and movingly reenacts God's great drama of redemption through Christ. The congregation's worship life is thus formed by two streams that become one river—sermons enriching season and season-enriching sermons.

At the very least the pastor should review the preaching schedule from the previous few years, set out the calendar of the entire year, consider the major seasons of the Christian year, and then determine sermons and sermon series for this year. To be sure, this preaching calendar will need to be reviewed and modified during the year, but the basic direction is set.

At this point others enter. They may include staff people responsible for worship planning, a worship coordinator, and a worship planning team. These "others" do not initiate the preaching plans but receive them and note how they are coordinated with the Christian year. What they receive is essentially a skeleton plan for the seasons of worship. Now it's time to put flesh on the bones, and the group gets larger. The yearly calendar is formed among the members of this group.

WHICH CALENDAR?

One basic question for worship planners is which calendar to observe. Four calendars vie for attention:

- *The chronological calendar.* The year begins in January and ends in December. It is possible to organize the church's life along these lines. In January we begin a new year and have a new calendar; in December we put it away.

Which Calendar?

- The chronological calendar
- The church-program calendar
- The "greeting card" calendar
- The Christian year calendar

- *The church-program calendar.* Instead of January through December, this calendar runs from September through August. In September we say, "Everybody's back." New classes and new schedules are established, and the calendar continues until late spring, when many activities slow down for the summer months—and then begin again in September. Should worship be planned on the basis of this essentially nine-month calendar?
- *The "greeting card" calendar.* We have attended churches where worship seems to be built around certain social and secular events like Mother's Day, Father's Day, Eagle Scout Day, perhaps Memorial Day, Independence Day, and other such observances. How much influence should these have? Should parts of the liturgy address these themes?
- *The Christian year calendar.* This pattern observes the reenactment of God's drama of redemption through the ministry of Christ. In this case the year begins in Advent (four weeks before Christmas) and continues through Pentecost, a season of growing, until we arrive back at the beginning of Advent.

Completely isolating these calendars from one another is virtually impossible. But we must clearly identify which will serve as our primary pattern and which will have secondary influence.

SHAPERS OF THE CALENDAR

Let's turn our attention to some of the considerations that shape the yearly worship calendar. We earlier spoke of our conviction that the Christian year should form the primary pattern and that other calendars should be secondary shapers. Let's take a closer look.

The Christian Year

We remember and celebrate God's actions best when we place them within time and history. God entered history with his acts of saving love, and so we should see those acts as within history. God told the Israelites that they should sacrifice the Passover lamb every year at a certain time of remembrance. Throughout Old Testament history the Israelites were taught to remember that God came *into time* to do his work. The ministry of Jesus all took place *within time*. Christ instituted the Lord's Supper on a specific Thursday evening for us to remember what occurred *in time*. His crucifixion and resurrection are not only doctrines and truths; they are historical events that occurred *in time*. He ascended into heaven at an identifiable *time*. The Holy Spirit was poured out on the church at a certain *time*. All these events happened *in time,* and the church should not divorce its remembrance of these events from the marking of time.

Therefore, the observance of the Christian year is theologically and practically the ideal starting point for structuring the seasonal worship calendar. The practice of the Christian year was developed in the early church. Evangelical and Reformed Protestants generally paid less attention to it, thereby losing many of its benefits. Now many of these churches are joining other Christians in its observance.

The focal points of the Christian year are the incarnation and the death and resurrection of Jesus Christ. Even the earliest Christians recognized that the resurrection of Christ began a "new time." The fact that two major events of the church took place during Jewish celebrations—Passover and Pentecost—helped the early Christians to link themselves with the Jewish reckoning of time. So, like the Jews, the early Christians marked time. However, unlike the Jews, they marked their time now by the events of the new age of fulfillment in Christ. These major moments are the incarnation and the death and resurrection of Christ. In these events all of time has a center.

The Christian year begins with Advent, a period of four weeks preceding the birth of Christ. Advent means "coming," and these weeks are filled with preparation, anticipation, and longing. Our angle of vision has a duel focus—on the arrival of the Christ child as the Messiah in Bethlehem and on the arrival of Christ at the end of time. While we still look forward to his second coming, the season of Advent as the anticipation of Christ's birth ends at Christmas.

Epiphany follows, referring to the manifestation of God's glory and light in Jesus Christ. In some traditions, Epiphany is less well known and observed in North America than other parts of the Christian year. This season begins on January 6 and can continue until Ash Wednesday. The season takes note of the visit of the Magi, the baptism of Christ, and his ministry; it ends with his transfiguration. Some communities of faith celebrate Epiphany as a day, some mark it over the course of a few weeks, and others extend the season to include all Sundays between Christmastide and Lent. For those who observe Epiphany as a brief season, the remainder of the season before Ash Wednesday is considered Ordinary Time.

Lent is the period of 40 days prior to Easter, excluding Sundays. The six weeks of Lent are usually a time of penitence with a focus on renewal and personal spiritual growth. In many congregations it is a time for catechumens (those being instructed) to make their preparations for baptism at Easter. The season begins on Ash Wednesday, when Christians are called to penitence, and culminates in the "Three Holy Days" of Maundy Thursday, Good Friday, and Holy Saturday.

Easter refers to a day and also to a season. Easter Sunday launches the season often called Eastertide, which continues to Pentecost. This time focuses on joy and celebration as we remember the resurrection of Christ, his postresurrection appearances, the coming of the kingdom of God, and his ascension to heaven.

Pentecost can also refer to both a day and a season. It is the 50th day after Easter and marks the outpouring of the Holy Spirit. As a season, it is the longest of the Christian calendar, beginning on Pentecost day, and continuing until Advent begins again. It is often labeled "Ordinary Time." Children are often taught to think of this as "Growing Time." Worship during this season focuses on the continued work of the resurrected Christ and the work of the Holy Spirit in empowering the church to do Christ's work in the world.

The entire cycle of the Christian year ends with Christ the King Sunday, always the last Sunday before a new Christian year begins with Advent. The church's worship on this Sunday focuses on the cosmic character of Christ's reign over the world. Then Advent begins again, and the cycle is repeated. You will find a useful summary of the Christian year at the end of this chapter. This annual cycle gives the worshiping congregation an excellent opportunity to mark the entire ministry of Jesus Christ each year and to build its worship around those events.

A similar method of structuring the Christian year has recently been proposed in *The Worship Sourcebook* (Grand Rapids: Baker Book House, Calvin Institute of Christian Worship, and Faith Alive Resources, 2004). Here the events of the Christian year are structured around the major professions of the Nicene Creed. Since the Nicene Creed is a widely known ecumenical creed of the Christian church, many traditions will find this pattern helpful (also at the end of the chapter). Organizing the yearly worship calendar around a historic creed enables a church to avoid locking the schedule into particular dates.

- The creed professes "W*e believe in one God,*" so the church focuses on creation, providence, and thanksgiving. Services centered on these themes will most likely take place during Ordinary Time.
- The creed professes, "*We believe . . . in one Lord Jesus Christ,*" so the church remembers the ministry of Christ through the major events of the Christian year from Advent through Pentecost, also including Christ the King Sunday. Services on these themes will, for the most part, come during Advent, Epiphany, Lent, and Eastertide.
- The creed professes "*And we believe in the Holy Spirit,*" so the church celebrates Pentecost, Trinity Sunday, the unity of the church, and the communion of the saints.

We have observed that most churches follow the pattern of the Christian year at least to some extent. The seasons of Advent and Lent, and the days of Christmas, Easter, and Pentecost are almost always part of the worship calendar. Beyond that, each church gives itself freedom to determine how thoroughly the various seasons should be observed and what other parts the year will be included.

True, such observances can to some seem only ceremonial and formal. Yet to retell the entire life and ministry of Christ each year is a powerful and rich foundation on which to build a season of worship.

The Lectionary

Worship planners from some traditions also use another resource in their work. They are familiar with and regularly follow the lectionary. The lectionary is a calendar of Scripture lessons for public reading in worship.

All Scripture passages are preselected and published as a three-year cycle. Different versions of the lectionary are used by various denominations, but all follow much the same pattern. Today Protestants are expressing an increasing appreciation for the lectionary. They see the benefits of a structured and balanced pattern of Scripture readings. And they also are coming to realize that such a calendar of preselected readings will expose the church to some passages of Scripture the pastor might not otherwise select. However, others have found that some key Scripture passages are omitted, that the suggested passages don't always fit together well, and that using the lectionary makes preaching through whole books of Scripture difficult. In 1992 the *Revised Common Lectionary* was published to correct some perceived weaknesses in previous publications. In each of the three yearly cycles, four Scripture passages are provided for each Sunday—an Old Testament reading, a Psalm reading, a New Testament reading from Acts or one of the letters, and a Gospel reading. Each year the Gospel readings come primarily from Matthew, Mark, and Luke; usually the readings are drawn from the Gospel of John during the Easter season. We have included a sampling of the *Revised Common Lectionary* here. Pastors and worship planners who use the lectionary are able to know years ahead what Scriptures will be read in services.

The Church Program

While the Christian year and the lectionary look complete and sufficient on paper, worship planners also need to consider the program of the local congregation as they plan their year. Every congregation observes particular events that are important to the life of the church. Undoubtedly there will be events in the local church program that need placement in the worship calendar or at least some attention in the liturgy, and worship planners are obligated to consider such matters. Perhaps there is a mission emphasis week or two, stewardship Sunday, a youth service, commissioning of staff, commissioning or installation of office-bearers, ordination of clergy, and certainly the celebration of the sacraments for congregations that do not observe them weekly. In addition, a seasonal calendar must take into consideration what happens in most churches during the summer months. When planners anticipate lower levels of regular attendance, it becomes necessary to plan worship with themes that can stand alone, rather than those that build from week to week.

Sampling of the Revised Common Lectionary

Year A	Year B	Year C
First Sunday of Advent Isaiah 2:1-5 Psalm 122 Romans 13:11-14 Matthew 24:36-44	Isaiah 64:1-9 Psalm 80:1-7, 17-19 I Corinthians 1:3-9 Mark 13:24-37	Jeremiah 33:14-16 Psalm 25:1-10 I Thessalonians 3:9-13 Luke 21:25-36
Second Sunday of Advent Isaiah 11:1-10 Psalm 72:1-7, 18,19 Romans 15:4-13 Matthew 3:1-12	Isaiah 40:1-11 Psalm 85:1-2, 8-13 II Peter 3:8-15 Luke 1:1-8	Malachi 3:1-4 Luke 1:68-79 Philippians 1:3-11 Luke 3:1-6
Third Sunday of Advent Isaiah 35:1-10 Psalm 146:5-10 James 5:7-10 Matthew 11:2-11	Isaiah 61:1-4, 8-11 Psalm 126 I Thessalonians 5:16-24 John 1:6-8, 19-28	Zephaniah 3:14-20 Isaiah 12:2-6 Philippians 4:4-7 Luke 3:7-18
Fourth Sunday of Advent Isaiah 7:10-16 Psalm 80:1-7, 17-19 Romans 1:1-7 Matthew 1:18-25	II Samuel 7:1-11, 16 Luke 1:47-55, or Psalm 89:1-4, 19-26 Romans 16:25-27 Luke 1:26-38	Micah 5:2-5 Luke 1:47-55, or Psalm 80:1-7 Hebrews 10:5-10 Luke 1:36-45
Christmas Eve Isaiah 9:2-7 Psalm 96 Titus 2:11-14 Luke 2:1-14 (15-20)	Isaiah 9:2-7 Psalm 96 Titus 2:11-14 Luke 2:1-14 (15-20)	Isaiah 9:2-7 Psalm 96 Titus 2:11-14 Luke 2:1-14 (15-20)
Christmas Day Isaiah 62:7-10 Psalm 98 Hebrews 1:1-4 (5-12) John 1:1-14	Isaiah 62:7-10 Psalm 98 Hebrews 1:1-4 (5-12) John 1:1-14	Isaiah 62:6-12 Psalm 98 Hebrews 1:1-4 (5-12) John 1:1-14

When all is considered, worship planners have a complex task. Structuring an entire year of worship requires taking into consideration more factors than first meet the eye. Yet the benefits far outweigh the challenges.

To aid you in the task, and to minimize the possibility of forgetting critical events, we've constructed a list of possible events for your consideration as you plan. You will notice that they are separated into two categories—Christian year observances and possible congregational observances. You will surely need to add others of your own.

Observances of the Christian year:

- Four Sundays of Advent Season
- Christmas Eve and/or Day
- Epiphany Sunday(s)
- Ash Wednesday
- Six Sundays of Lent
- Passion or Palm Sunday
- Maundy Thursday
- Good Friday
- Easter Vigil
- Easter
- Ascension Day
- Pentecost
- Trinity Sunday
- All Saints Day
- Christ the King Sunday

Congregational Observances
- Baptism
- Holy Communion Sundays
- New Year's Eve or Day
- Sanctity of Human Life Sunday/Celebration of Life
- Stewardship Sundays
- Mission emphasis Sundays
- Youth Sunday
- National Day of Prayer

- Honoring of graduates
- Commissioning of church staff members
- Commissioning or installation of office-bearers
- Ordination of clergy
- Prayers for the persecuted church
- World Communion Sunday
- Week of Prayer for Christian Unity
- Reformation Day
- Thanksgiving Day
- Church anniversary
- Other local events

It's obvious that planning teams will have much to keep in mind. We have provided several planning sheets and sample schedules as helpful tools at the end of the chapter.

When to Prepare the Calendar

We've tried to establish the benefit of making such a calendar and to identify the key participants and the influences that shape its formation. We've made the case that worship planners should not live week to week or even month to month but rather should take a look at a 12-month span and see the entire year as a journey. But the questions remain—when should this be done and how much lead time is necessary?

What Stephen Rummage, associate pastor of preaching at Southeastern Baptist Theological Seminary, Wake Forest, North Carolina, says about sermon planning can also be said of worship planning: "In most cases, the longest workable plan is the one-year plan" and "The shortest plan is the 13-week, or quarterly, plan" (Rummage, "The Mechanics of Sermon Planning," *Preaching*, Sept.-Oct. 2003, 29-30; or Rummage, *Planning Your Preaching* [Grand Rapids: Kregel Publications, 2002]). We agree that the quarterly plan of only 13 weeks is minimally adequate and that planning for an entire year as a unit is a much better choice.

Worship planners we have consulted find that their planning is usually done in three stages, with each stage becoming more detailed than the previous. *Stage 1* is the long-range planning that sketches out the entire year. This is perhaps the most challenging because it requires a 12-month overview and most people tend not to think long term. It is still wisest to begin at this stage. *Stage 2*, or medium-range planning, breaks the entire year into several segments—usually September through January, January through May, and the summer months of June through August. More detailed planning is done for each of the segments in this stage. *Stage 3* involves much more specific planning for each month and then, of course, for each week. Everyone does detailed planning to one degree or another; some do medium-range planning; but our research and experience indicate that fewer do long-range planning.

It may be daunting to look ahead an entire year and anticipate what worship should encompass 10 months from now. However, planning in stages 2 and 3 will take a clearer direction if stage 1 planning is done thoughtfully. One pastor wrote that he takes a week in June every year to plan through to the next June. In that way all energies can be focused on the seasonal planning process without interruption. Another pastor takes a week in January to chart out the long-range planning for her entire calendar year. In churches with multiple staff sharing the responsibility for worship, it's more difficult to set aside an entire week and so a brainstorming and planning retreat for a couple of days may occur several times during the year.

Though it will take special effort to find a block of time for such a retreat, doing so is a necessary first step. The effort should include several ingredients—the approval of others such as the church board, freedom from all pastoral duties except emergencies, freedom from preaching the following Sunday, and a quiet place where reflection and planning can be done without distraction. We have found it helpful to inform the congregation that a planning week is scheduled and to ask their prayers for God's direction in the work. Some pastors find they are able to find a quiet location away from church such as a cottage or cabin; others have gone to a retreat center; and still others have found a quiet corner in a local college library—or Starbucks! The pastor should take along the record of preaching of the previous three years, notes and files of ideas for preaching during the coming season, and all pertinent information about events to be observed during the year. With leisure time for study, reflection, and prayer, the pastor will often find the Spirit of God moving quietly, and sometimes slowly, while the season takes shape.

Some find that a week once a year is sufficient. Others prefer to schedule such a retreat week at multiple intervals during the year. We have found that during a week in the summer, either July or August, we can chart out the entire seasonal schedule. We have found it wise to use June to recover from the fatigue of the program year, as well as that of Holy Week and Easter, and then we feel ready to plan creatively during July and August. Others prefer to plan in June and use the rest of the quiet summer months to flesh out the initial plans. Then, during a shorter retreat in January, they will review plans and make them more specific for the next few months. The summer months' plans can be given that same attention during the week after Easter. A healthy and comfortable rhythm develops—a week to chart the entire year and shorter, more frequent planning sessions to review, update, and refine plans.

THE PROCESS OF SEASONAL CALENDAR PREPARATION

For some pastors, scheduling the retreat week for planning is the greatest difficulty. For others, the challenge is to develop a method for planning. Pastors may agree that this stage 1 planning is necessary, and may even have the full blessing of their church board to set aside a week's retreat for such planning, yet their work style is such that they don't know where to begin or how to use their time efficiently. In the interest of helping such people, we lay out a process developed through the years of our ministries. Pastors will want to adapt this process to fit their own situations and work styles, but a strategy similar to this will make a retreat week more valuable and satisfying. Here are the steps to follow:

1. *Commit yourself to prayer.* We must deepen our awareness of our dependence on the Holy Spirit for the work of worship planning. Even the best strategies and most productive study times will not bear good fruit unless the Holy Spirit is moving through them. Some may hesitate to engage in long-range planning out of fear that it may stifle the Holy Spirit's leading. Such worries are needless. The Holy Spirit is as fully active in the planning process as in the immediate actions of each week. Submit the entire week of planning and the entire year to be planned to the Spirit's care! Those who do often discover that the Spirit anticipates the pastoral needs of the congregation long before the pastors are aware of them. Remember the

pastor who found the Holy Spirit directing his sermon plans even before the events of 9/11?

2. *Collect information and impressions to take along.* Preachers must obviously know the Word of God to preach it faithfully, but they must also know the needs of the congregation and the community. Preacher-planners should bring several resources that provide the necessary information for this first planning session—the worship and preaching schedule of the past three years, the resource file of ideas collected as possible preaching material for the coming year, impressions gleaned during pastoral work about the life and needs of the congregation, input from the church board or elders about what they perceive as current congregational and community needs, and suggestions solicited from the congregation. All these resources will be highly valuable for a planning session.

3. *Set out the yearly worship calendar.* Refer to the planning sheets at the end of this chapter, which you may find helpful. Chart out all 52 Sundays, including notations about the seasons of the Christian year and the dates on which they occur. Be sure the calendar is large enough to accommodate more information as it becomes available.

4. *Chart out the festival days and observances.* Once you have begun with the major seasons of the Christian year, add the dates for the Lord's Supper if your congregation does not celebrate it weekly, and other special days your congregation observes, as noted above. Try to make this listing as complete as possible. It will greatly influence the worship and sermon themes you select.

5. *Select and chart out your sermons and sermon series.* As you plan, determine how carefully you will follow the lectionary. Then determine whether you will preach a series of sermons on key scriptural doctrines shaped by the confessions of the church. Then select and fill in the series of messages you will have for Advent, Epiphany, Lent, and other major seasons. (When we refer to a series of sermons, we have in mind a sequence preached over several weeks, developed along similar themes or a common focus.) Don't forget to include your vacations and other times when you will be away. If you have both morning and evening worship, take note of which sermons or series will be preached in the morning and which in the evening. It is not necessary at this point to have the entire series of

The Process for a Planning Retreat

1. Commit yourself to prayer
2. Collect information and impressions to take along
3. Set out the seasonal worship calendar
4. Chart out the festival days and observances
5. Chart out sermons and sermon series
6. Identify service themes
7. Share the schedule
8. Set up files for each sermon series and season
9. Set up planning files for each Sunday of the year

sermons charted out in detail, but only the series identified, the number of weeks needed, and the weeks blocked in.

6. *Identify service themes.* Each worship service should have a clearly identified theme so that planning can be focused. The theme for each service should be spelled out in one relatively brief phrase or sentence and noted on the planning sheet for that week. The themes for the major seasons of the Christian year will be determined by both the seasonal observance and the sermon scheduled for that day. For other services the event observed and the sermon will shape the theme. When this planning calendar is sent to others, it will be much more helpful if such themes are included for their planning.

7. *Share the schedule.* Once all this has been put together, it's time to return to the office and begin the process of sharing the schedule. An overview of the entire year is the most important item to put in the hands of others. Worship committee members should see it at their next meeting so they can begin their work. The elders or church board should be interested in seeing it for information. The worship planning team members certainly need it so their involvement in the process can begin. Any special assistants such as artists, musicians, and others will be pleased to know the direction of the year in worship so they can begin their planning.

8. *Set up files for each sermon series and season.* A resource file for a season or a series of sermons becomes an "incubator." A file folder set up to collect ideas, quotations, illustrations, and liturgical elements such as litanies proves very useful over the months. If you

pick up ideas and illustrations at unexpected times and places, you will have a place to keep track of them.

9. *Set up planning files for each Sunday of the year.* We have used a three-ring binder containing the yearly chart. We included sheets on which we could collect ideas and suggestions that would be helpful in stage 3 of the planning process. Many churches will want to use computer technology for this step and create computer files for worship planning. These can be shared by all worship planners so that each can add ideas for upcoming services. Obviously, you will want to set up a password to protect the computer files so that they are accessible only to the planners and any other authorized users. Many planners will find it helpful to maintain both computer files and hard copies.

Maybe this idea of planning an entire year is new to you. Or maybe it's been a dream that you haven't quite been able to pull off. It's a wise and helpful practice to develop. Worship planning will become more enjoyable. The worship life of the church will become more thoughtful. The Spirit of God will have plenty of room to work and lead. And teams of people will be able to work together more enjoyably.

So go for it! Stretch yourself! Take a whole year into view at one time. Learn some new habits that include long-range planning. We think you'll be glad you did.

Overview of the Christian Year

The Christian Year is organized around the two major cycles of Christ's redemptive work on earth: the Christmas Cycle (Advent, Christmas, and Epiphany) and the Easter Cycle (Lent, Easter, Pentecost). Each cycle has a period of preparation, the festival(s) of celebration, and a following "ordinary" or "growing" season in which Christians live out the implications of the incarnation, death, and resurrection of Christ and the work of the Holy Spirit.

A fairly standard set of liturgical colors is used ecumenically for each of these seasons. For example, many churches use purple in Advent because of its penitential or royal associations; others use blue to suggest expectation or to link Advent to baptism. Gold and white are often used for Epiphany because they are suggestive of light or the royal gifts given by the magi. Some quickly replace the Epiphany colors with green for Ordinary Time or Growing Season until Lent begins. In Lent the color is purple, suggesting penitence. It is often changed to red for Holy Week to remind us of the atoning sacrifice of Christ. Then it changes to white or gold for the Easter season to represent celebration of the victory of Christ. The color of Pentecost is red for the fire of the Holy Spirit. Green is the the color during the ensuing Ordinary Time. White is often used for Trinity Sunday and Christ the King Sunday. Such colors signal the changing mood of each season and are valuable nonverbal forms of communication within the worship space.

Many ecumenically accepted symbols are in use for each of these seasons. We encourage you to explore and make use of them. You will find helpful resources in *Worship Without Words—The Signs and Symbols of Our Faith,* by Patricia S. Klein (Brewster, Mass.: Paraclete Press, 2000). Online resources on Christian symbols can be found at http://home.att.net/ ~wegast/symbols/symbols.htm.

Many churches find that the colors and symbols of the season are especially helpful to young children and that the motivation to use such colors and symbols comes from the children's ministries. They become excellent teaching tools for children—and their parents.

THE CHRISTMAS CYCLE

Advent Season

The color is blue or purple.
- The first Sunday of Advent to the fourth Sunday of Advent

Christmas Season

The color is white or gold.
- Christmas Eve or Christmas Day
- First Sunday after Christmas
- Epiphany of the Lord (January 6)

Season after Epiphany

The color is green. (Note: in some traditions this is called Epiphany season and begins with Epiphany. Some prefer to call this season Ordinary Time.)
- First Sunday after Epiphany—the Baptism of the Lord
- Second Sunday after Epiphany to the eighth Sunday after Epiphany (depending on when Lent begins)
- Last Sunday of Epiphany season—the Transfiguration of the Lord

THE EASTER CYCLE

Lenten Season

The color is purple, with red as an alternative for Holy Week.
- Ash Wednesday
- First Sunday of Lent through the fifth Sunday of Lent
- Holy Week
  Beginning with Passion or Palm Sunday
  Maundy Thursday
  Good Friday
  Holy Saturday—Easter Vigil
  (Note: The *triduum,* or "three great days"—Maundy Thursday, Good Friday, and Holy Saturday—form a unit.)

Easter Season

The color is white or gold.
- Easter Vigil (note that the Vigil bridges the seasons of Lent and Easter)
- Easter
- Second Sunday of Eastertide through the sixth Sunday of Eastertide
- Ascension Day
- Seventh Sunday of Eastertide

Pentecost Season

The color is red.
- Pentecost Sunday

The Season after Pentecost (also called "Ordinary Time")

- Trinity Sunday—the first Sunday after Pentecost (the color is usually white)
- Sundays after Pentecost (the color is green)
- Christ the King Sunday—usually the final Sunday of the Christian year before Advent resumes (the color usually is white)

THE CHRISTIAN YEAR ACCORDING TO THE NICENE CREED

It is possible to structure commonly celebrated events in the Christian year around the basic professions of the ecumenical Nicene Creed. This structure is suggested by *The Worship Sourcebook* (Grand Rapids: Baker Book House, Calvin Institute of Christian Worship, and Faith Alive Resources, 2004). Many resources for the worship service are provided for each of these observances of the Christian year in this book.

We believe in one God.

- Creation
- Providence
- Thanksgiving

We believe . . . in one Lord Jesus Christ.

- Advent
- Christmas
- Epiphany
- Baptism of the Lord
- Transfiguration of the Lord
- Ash Wednesday
- Lent
- Passion or Palm Sunday
- Maundy Thursday
- Good Friday
- Easter
- Ascension of the Lord
- Christ the King Sunday

And we believe in the Holy Spirit.

- Pentecost
- Trinity Sunday
- Unity of the Church
- Communion of the Saints

SEASONAL PLANNING SHEETS

Christmas Cycle Planning Sheet

Date	Christian Year	Scripture	Theme
	First Sunday of Advent		
	Second Sunday of Advent		
	Third Sunday of Advent		
	Fourth Sunday of Advent		
	Christmas Eve/Day		
	First Sunday after Christmas		
	Epiphany of our Lord		
	First Sunday after Epiphany		
	Second Sunday after Epiphany		
	Third Sunday after Epiphany		
	Fourth Sunday after Epiphany		
	Fifth Sunday after Epiphany		
	Sixth Sunday after Epiphany		
	Seventh Sunday after Epiphany		
	Eighth Sunday after Epiphany		

Easter Cycle Planning Sheet

Date	Christian Year	Scripture	Theme
	AshWednesday		
	First Sunday in Lent		
	Second Sunday in Lent		
	Third Sunday in Lent		
	Fourth Sunday in Lent		
	Fifth Sunday in Lent		
	Passion or Palm Sunday		
	Maundy Thursday		
	Holy Saturday		
	Easter Sunday		
	Second Sunday of Eastertide		
	Third Sunday of Eastertide		
	Fourth Sunday of Eastertide		
	Fifth Sunday of Eastertide		
	Sixth Sunday of Eastertide		
	Ascension Day		
	Seventh Sunday of Eastertide		
	Pentecost		
	Trinity Sunday		

SAMPLE WORKSHEET FOR SEASONAL WORSHIP PLANNING

Date	Morning	Evening
	Preaching: Sermon: Scripture: Theme: Season: Lead Musician: Music Ministry: Special Events:	Preaching: Sermon: Scripture: Theme: Season: Lead Musician: Music Ministry: Special Events:
	Preaching: Sermon: Scripture: Theme: Season: Lead Musician: Music Ministry: Special Events:	Preaching: Sermon: Scripture: Theme: Season: Lead Musician: Music Ministry: Special Events:
	Preaching: Sermon: Scripture: Theme: Season: Lead Musician: Music Ministry: Special Events:	Preaching: Sermon: Scripture: Theme: Season: Lead Musician: Music Ministry: Special Events:

Note that the following is the information needed for each service:

1. *Preaching*: the pastor who is responsible for the sermon in this service.
2. *Sermon*: the title of the message.
3. *Scripture*: the passages from which the sermon will be derived.
4. *Theme:* a brief statement of the theme of this service as shaped by the sermon and the season.
5. *Season*: the event in the Christian year to be observed.
6. *Lead musician*: the musician responsible for selecting service music and leading the congregation.
7. *Music ministry:* other persons or groups who will be providing music ministry during the service.
8. *Special Events:* sacraments or other observances to be included in the service.

Future Dates on the Liturgical Calendar

Dates for major Christian observances for future years are given for your reference. Please note that each liturgical year starts with Advent in the preceeding calendar year (e.g., Year A, which takes place mainly in 2005, begins November 28, 2004).

Year	Advent Begins	Lent Begins (Ash Wed.)	Eastertide Begins	Pentecost
2005 A	November 28	February 9	March 27	May 15
2006 B	November 27	March 1	April 16	June 4
2007 C	December 3	February 21	April 8	May 27
2008 A	December 2	February 6	March 23	May 11
2009 B	November 30	February 25	April 12	May 31
2010 C	November 29	February 17	April 4	May 23
2011 A	November 28	March 9	April 24	June 12
2012 B	November 27	February 22	April 8	May 27
2013 C	December 2	February 13	March 31	May 19
2014 A	December 1	March 5	April 20	June 8
2015 B	November 30	February 18	April 5	May 24
2016 C	November 29	February 10	March 27	May 15
2017 A	November 27	March 1	April 16	June 4
2018 B	December 3	February 14	April 1	May 20
2019 C	December 2	March 6	April 21	June 9

CHAPTER 5

WEEKLY WORSHIP PLANNING

If you ask Doug about his experiences in worship planning, he's likely to break into a big smile and tell you that he feels blessed. "I work with a dream worship planning team," he'll say. And then he'll go on to explain, "Our time together is satisfying. We know each other well and care for each other, we think in much the same terms, and we respect each other. When we get together we work productively, nego-tiate differences, and even share a few jokes and stories. But we also work hard and play off each other's ideas. Not only do we plan good worship, but we have a delightful time." Doug acknowledges that the time must come when the group's membership will change, with in-evitable adjustments, and that he is already grieving that day!

Rosa's worship planning group is much different from Doug's. Rosa loves worship planning and finds rich satisfaction in designing wor-ship services. So do the others in the group. But lately their planning meetings have become frustrating. Five members of Trinity Church meet weekly to contribute their insights and gifts. But one of the mem-bers has become increasingly negative. Most listen to each other well and work through their differing ideas. But Clark just sits there with his arms folded while the discussion unfolds, and then finally states flatly, "That just won't work. It just doesn't flow!" His words silence others and kill discussion. Rosa senses that both the quality of the team's work and their joy in doing it is slipping away. She's surprised that one person's negative comments can erode the spirit of the whole group.

Juanita and Angela are responsible for planning the worship services at Clear Valley Church. Angela is the pastor, Juanita the part-time worship coordinator. They are committed to the worship life of Clear Valley Church, but neither is disciplined in scheduling her time. Angela finds that the tasks of ministry include frequent interruptions; it's hard to establish a weekly schedule and stick to it. Juanita assumes that because she's a part-time employee, the planning time can be determined by her own weekly schedule. They chuckle about "catch-as-catch-can" worship planning. They always manage to have the Sunday service ready, but not without harried last-minute tasks. The one who pays the price for their work style, however, is Judy, the church secretary, who must prepare the bulletin and worship sheets and relay the information to other worship leaders. Sometimes Judy is handed a large task on Friday afternoon shortly before she'd like to leave to pick up her children from school. And she feels the sting of absorbing flak from others who also end up having to do last-minute preparation. Last week she had to come in on Saturday to get things ready for Sunday. Judy's getting pretty weary of this pattern.

We have already established that a worship planning team is in place and that it understands its role. All team members know the importance of collaboration. They're committed to a rich and vital worship life for their church. The congregation's theology of worship has been spelled out, and they agree in their views on worship. They've been working with the pastor to chart out the worship calendar for an entire year.

Now we turn our attention to the all-important weekly planning session. Though most members of the congregation will hardly be aware of these weekly sessions, their worship will be greatly influenced by what happens there.

AN EFFECTIVE TEAM GATHERS

In chapter 1 we dealt with the qualifications of worship team members, and in chapter 2 we addressed ways the planning team could be structured. Imagine now that we have the opportunity to observe and learn from a planning session of an effective team. What will we see?

One of the first things we'll notice is the spirit in which group members approach their work, taking worship planning seriously. For them it's not merely a task to be carried out, but a ministry to be fulfilled. A spirit of reverence and privilege seems to saturate the sessions. A holy sense of anticipation prevails about what will happen Sunday when the congregation gathers to meet God. One worship planner articulates the thoughts of many: "Planning worship is itself worship for me!"

We'll also notice that they have the congregation clearly in mind. A high level of awareness and sensitivity is evident among these worship planners. They know this congregation is diverse and multigenerational, and in their mind's eye they see the children, the youth, the young parents, and the older adults. Each generation must be considered. The planners are also attuned to various needs within the congregation. It's obvious they know the congregation well and have been in close relationship with many during the past week. They know some will be coming to worship to express gratitude and joy for a good week; others will be hurting because it's been a hard week; still others need to find forgiveness for failures. Some will be secure in their faith, some doubting, and others on the edge of cynicism. Some will come needing support, and others will be strong. It seems that the planning group can envision all of these people in their pews as it plans.

As we watch them work, their healthy relationships capture our attention. Here are people who respect each other, like to be together, and find it easy to exchange ideas and suggestions. They don't become defensive when others raise questions about their suggestions; they don't seem to get caught in "turf protection." They are willing to bend and easily defer to one another without feeling slighted. And they do it graciously. We notice that these relationships create synergy, so that the whole becomes greater than the sum of its parts. We can see why Doug, in the opening example, found his team's work as a group so satisfying and why Rosa found the opposite.

We're also struck by the high degree of discernment we see among this team. When it debates issues and questions about worship services, it is able to deal with them on the basis of principle and core values. Team members are not stuck on popular preferences, but on what is biblical, what best reflects their theology of worship, and what will best lead the

---

Marks of an Effective Team

1. A healthy spirit
2. An awareness of others' needs
3. Respectful relationships
4. Biblical discernment
5. Necessary resources
6. Sufficient time

---

congregation to engage with God. As we watch them, we know this congregation is blessed to have such a group planning its worship.

And then we notice that each has brought resources to the work. Not only have they brought their own knowledge of Christian worship, but they've also brought the fruit of their homework. The key planners provided in advance the schedule for the whole year, so all can see the big picture. The pastor has prepared a preaching schedule, along with Scripture passages, and a summary of the intent of Sunday's sermon. The musicians have done their research, and the choir director has come with a list of hymn suggestions and has prepared anthems consistent with the theme of the service. The other musicians are ready to contribute their ideas about where each of these can best be placed in the liturgy.

But something else catches our attention. We don't notice it at first, but as we watch the group members at work, we notice that they are not in a hurry. No one wants to rush in, get the job done in record time, and quickly get on to other things. They know this work will take time. They have learned that you can't rush creative efforts. A sense of holy leisure permeates the room. They are willing to give the Holy Spirit time to move among them as they work, even if he may move a little more slowly than their own preferred pace of life. Sufficient time is a key ingredient in this mix, and they've made that time available in their schedule.

THE TIMELINE OF PLANNING

To be sure, this work is time consuming. And because it is, we've found it helpful to sketch out a general timeline to shape the expectations of those who participate.

Annual Planning

As we explained in chapter 4, the pastor should take the lead in charting out the map for a year of preaching. Some are obviously more comfortable than others with working that far ahead, but those on the planning team will be in a better position to plan well if this preliminary work is done. If the pastor doesn't take the lead, it won't likely be done, and the planning work will be more difficult for all.

As we saw in chapter 4, planning is done during the summer months so that all planners have a clear idea in September of the entire year of worship. This schedule will take into consideration the Christian year and other necessary observances in the life of the congregation. Now when this annual plan is shared with others, brainstorming can begin about smaller seasonal segments of the year, and groups and ensembles can be assigned to participate in certain services—for example, musical groups, drama groups, and liturgical dance groups.

Preliminary Research

Once the pastor has put this annual worship calendar together and shared it with others, all team members should begin their own research and preparation. The minister of music, worship coordinator, or praise team leader can search for appropriate hymns and songs from a variety of sources. Choir directors can search the literature for good anthems, and order them if they're not in the choral library. The drama team can begin to look for dramas they'd like to use in worship. The visual arts team can brainstorm about banners. When several people are doing preliminary research on their specialties, they'll all come to a planning session with valuable suggestions and materials. At the end of this chapter is a sample Weekly Worship Planning Guide that can be reproduced for team members to use in preparing for the weekly meeting. It's helpful for most of this preliminary research to be done two or three months ahead of a given service.

Planning Meeting

The planning meeting is the intersection at which all these efforts come together. Team members will serve better if they give attention to the preparation of their hearts. Their own practice of the presence of God, confession and repentance, devotional meditations on Scripture, and prayer will enable them to prepare vital worship. In other words, what they are when they arrive at the team meeting will influence how they can serve.

We have found that some groups meet during the day, others over the supper hour, and some in the evening. The meeting time is determined by the number of people involved and their availability. Most of the worship planners with whom we've consulted have found that planning for each worship service requires an average of three to five hours. Those who follow denominationally provided liturgies will need less time. Those who must write their own and have an open field to do so will need this much time. Those who have two different services each Sunday will usually need to double that time.

Planning should be done far enough in advance that the work is not marred by last-minute scrambling. We believe it's best if the planning meeting for a specific service takes place approximately 10 days before the service is scheduled, and that the fine-tuning is wrapped up by Thursday morning of the week in which the service will take place, unless printing schedules require it earlier. The discipline to keep such a schedule will avoid many difficulties. Juanita and Angela, whose story is told at the opening of this chapter, had fallen victims to undisciplined schedules, and their work suffered for it.

The team that plans should also review and evaluate the previous week's service before beginning the planning for a new service. After this review the group turns its attention to the service(s) to be prepared. The primary goal of this session is to create a unified liturgy that, with a minimum of fine-tuning, is ready for print. The pastor should set the general theme of the service before the group. The Scripture passages to be used should be cited. Special events to be observed in worship will be noted at this time. Members of the group will contribute the results of their individual homework in their areas of expertise—providing songs, anthems, litanies, Scriptures and Scripture dramas, and so on. The "Sample Agenda for a Worship Planning Team" (at the end of chapter 2) outlines the steps to be followed. When the group nears the end of its meeting, members agree on dividing up the tasks that need to be done after the meeting.

It is also helpful to spend some time looking ahead to future services before the meeting adjourns. The team should have several worship services in various stages of development at any given time. Doing so avoids starting from scratch each week. When the service of the week is completed, the team turns its attention to other services—first the service details for the upcoming week, and then the services two or more weeks out. Members review the themes, raise any concerns they've encountered in research, and remind themselves of matters that will likely need attention before next week's meeting. Most worship planners that we've consulted prefer to have a month of worship services in various stages of development at any time.

Fine-Tuning

Not all will be finished when the meeting of the planning team is adjourned. Editing will be necessary before the service plan is ready for print. In some churches a completed service plan will be available only to worship leaders; in other churches it will be made available to all worshipers either on paper or projected on a screen. If you provide materials for the congregation, what they receive must be clear and accurate. Carelessness will quickly show! Perhaps copyright permissions must be included; texts of anthems or songs might be printed; litanies may need editing. Then all the details must be double-checked. This worship material should be meticulously proofread by two sets of eyes—preferably by readers other than those who have written and typed it. After any corrections are made and checked, it is finally ready for printing or projecting.

ISSUES THAT SHAPE THE SERVICE

Planning teams should also give attention to the large questions and issues that significantly shape worship. Such issues need to permeate all the discussion in the planning process; this attention will make a great difference in the spirit of the service.

One issue is the purpose of worship. Worship is an engagement with God. We are not designing a concert to entertain or to inspire an audience. Worship is a holy event in which God and his people converse. Our first purpose is not to "get something out of worship" but to extend to God glory and adoration. Though providing inspiration and nurture for worshipers is important, it is secondary.

We should also consider our intent. Are we designing this service for those who are already committed to a relationship with God, for those who are seeking, or both? Is it our intent to comfort people who may be feeling stress and pain, to stir those who may be too comfortable, to guide those seeking God, or to challenge worshipers to a greater level of obedience to God? Do we want to educate people in Christian truth, inspire their hearts and stir their emotions, or challenge them to make new commitments? While our purpose in worship will remain constant, our intent may change from week to week.

Scripture selections also shape our worship. Which passages are selected for reading and preaching, and how many passages are included—these are decisions that matter. The pastor will benefit from a regular analysis of the Scripture passages selected for preaching. How often do Old Testament passages provide the text for the sermon? How often do the Gospels? And the remainder of the New Testament? Similar questions should be asked about the Scripture readings used in other parts of the worship service. Are the people hearing the whole range of the Scriptures? Following, or at least consulting, the lectionary can be a valuable aid to ensure balance. Before a worship service is put in final print form, this issue needs to be addressed.

Another issue is the pastoral nature of worship. A congregation's culture and circumstances will shape its worship. Its worship life must be expressive of both its inner soul and its outer journey of faith. A worship service planned for a conference festival where worshipers do not know each other will differ from Sunday worship in, for example, the three congregations cited at the opening of this chapter.

The worship planning team for a given congregation must understand that worship may be different here than it would be in another congregation. And worship may need to be different here this week than it was a month ago. Pastors must take all of these differences into consideration if they are to preach sermons that are pastorally sensitive. And worship planners must do the same as they construct liturgies. The team will carefully select songs, create litanies, choose readings, and write prayers with a pastoral awareness of the community's experiences and needs. One pastor cites the comment of a worshiper who felt that the messages often uniquely connected with her: "Pastor, who do you write your sermons for when I'm not here?" The worship planning team must aim for that connectedness.

In the planning session the team will need to look inside the life of the worshiping community, developing an awareness of the needs and issues worshipers bring with them. Will children be present? Will youth be there?

Young families? Seniors? The team must also look outside the congregation. What recent events in the community, nation, and world will have touched their hearts and minds this week? What positive events will stir their thanks? What kinds of anxieties and struggles can we expect to be present? What spiritual issues are affecting the life of this community, positively or negatively? Drawing in these pastoral concerns will shape the worship that is planned.

Another "shaping" issue concerns the selection of healthy music. The voice of the people will most often take the form of song. Therefore, the selection of music for the service is a key element in shaping the service. Music has historically had a prominent place in the worship of God's people. When we make music, we stand in a long line of those who have entered God's presence with music—from chanted Psalms to the canticles of the early church, to Reformation hymnody and the contemporary hymns and choruses of the present century. We all know the power of music to move the human spirit, a power that can be negative or positive, manipulating or inspiring us, and helping us to breathe our sighs and prayers.

Kennon Callahan, an interdenominational church consultant, makes a sweeping and, we believe, accurate claim for music in worship:

> Music contributes 40 percent of the service's power and impact, its movement and momentum. I have been known to say that when my own preaching is off, I count on the music to carry the service. I have worked with many excellent pastors, good shepherds, wise, caring leaders, whose preaching—rated on a scale of one to ten—was realistically a seven. Surrounded by music that is dynamic and inspiring, the congregation hears the preaching as a nine. When the music isn't contributing its usual share, the pastor's preaching is perceived as only a five. [Callahan, *Dynamic Worship—Mission, Grace, Praise, and Power* (HarperSanFrancisco, 1994), 30-31]

Planners should be aware of the power of music, but also conversant with the many types of music that could be included in worship. The service music of prelude, offertory, and postlude should direct the worshiper in a way that is consistent with the theme of the service and the flow of the liturgy. The ministry of music within the service, given on behalf of the congregation by choirs or individuals, instrumental or vocal, needs to do the same. The preparation of these is usually well underway before the weekly planning session, which will focus on congregational song. Some songs help us express our praise, adoration, and thanksgiving. Others proclaim the story of God's acts and our testimonies of faith. Others enable us to give expression to our pain and sorrow or to confess our sinfulness. Still others help us to breathe out our sense of hope and anticipation for the future. We have found that multiple minds give a more balanced perspective to this task.

CREATING AN ORDER OF WORSHIP

Let's look more closely at the work of this planning team as it meets. Once the material is before the participants and they know the theme of the service, work begins in earnest. Each person will have an opportunity to contribute suggestions in his or her area of expertise. But the basic issue to address first is the pattern or order of the service into which the elements of worship will be placed. A planning team must consider how it can best implement the basic "Principles for Worship as Dialogue" and formulate its expression into a workable pattern.

Principles for Worship as Dialogue

1. Worship is a corporate conversation between God and his children.
2. Worship happens at God's gracious invitation.
3. The major activity of worship happens on the vertical dimension.
4. God speaks to us in the greeting, the pardon, the reading of Scripture, the sermon, and the blessing.
5. We speak to God in prayer, confession, affirmations of faith, and song.
6. Preaching, as the proclamation of God's word, is central to worship.
7. Christ comes to us in the celebration of the sacraments.
8. Congregational song is the voice of the people.
9. Worship engages the intellect and understanding.
10. Worship includes the whole range of emotion.
11. Worship reflects our oneness with the global church.
12. Obedience to God in all of life is the desired fruit of worship.

There is a historic pattern of worship that expresses these principles and is worth careful consideration. Some churches follow it closely, others revise or adapt it to fit their local situation; still others follow no set pattern at all, although it seems that in most congregations a pattern does gradually develop, whether deliberate or not!

We always began with the basic assumption that worship is a corporate engagement with God, a group dialogue or conversation with him. "Engagement" is a term used by David Peterson, a respected author and principal of Oak Hill College, a theological school in London. He says in his book *Engaging with God* (Downers Grove, Ill.: InterVarsity Press, 1992), "[T]he worship of the living and true God is essentially *an engagement with him on the terms that he proposes and in the way that he alone makes possible*" (20). In some parts of the liturgy God speaks to us, primarily through his word, and in other parts of the liturgy we speak to God through such acts as our prayers and songs. Many Christian traditions follow a pattern of worship whose roots go back many centuries. Worship then includes the Gathering, the Renewal, the Service of the Word, the Service of Response, either with or without the Table of the Lord, and the Dismissal. This pattern of worship is made clear in the chart on the following page.

This grid helps us to visualize the pattern of worship (first column), provides an explanation of the purpose of each movement (second column), and lists elements that might be included in each section (third column). The third column intends to mention all (or most) possible elements, though we realize that not every church includes all of these things every week. Not all selections of the service will require an equal amount of time. Nor will the time allotted to each section be the same from week to week.

The Planning Process

1. The pastor presents information on Scripture readings and sermon for the service.
2. The group agrees on the overall theme for the service.
3. Team members contribute their suggestions for worship elements such as hymns and songs, anthems, litanies, and dramas.
4. Other special events for the service are considered.
5. The team finalizes the elements of the worship service.
6. The team arranges the elements into an order of worship.
7. The team walks through the structured service to sense its flow and to note transitions.
8. Tasks still needing completion are assigned.

The Pattern of Worship

Movement	Purpose	Possible Elements
The Gathering	The corporate conversation between God and his children is begun. God's children are entering his presence and the dialogue begins.	Prelude Processional The Call to Worship Opening Litany/Sentences Our Declaration of Trust God's Greeting Songs Introits Anthems Passing the Peace Liturgical Dance
The Renewal	As worshipers come into the presence of a holy God, they acknowledge their sinfulness and seek forgiveness and renewal in God's grace.	The Call to Confession The Prayer of Confession The Assurance of Pardon Response of Gratitude Reading God's Will for Our Obedience Sacrament of Baptism Remembering Our Baptism Passing the Peace
The Word	God's Word is proclaimed, so that his voice is heard and his people are instructed and strengthened.	The Children's Moment The Reading of Scripture The Prayer for Illumination Song of Preparation The Sermon The Prayer of Application Anthem Scripture Drama
The Response to God's Word	God's Word always calls for a response on the part of those who hear. This section provides opportunities for responses of faith, thanksgiving, and obedience.	Songs Anthems Prayers Offerings Expression of Commitment Profession of the Creed or other affirmations of faith Liturgical Dance Drama
The Lord's Supper	A major response of God's people to his Word is our participation in the body and blood of our Lord.	Songs Words of Invitation Great Prayer of Thanksgiving Participating in the Bread Participating in the Cup Profession of the Creed
The Dismissal	The corporate conversation between God and his people comes to an end, and elements are provided by which we take leave of each other. The dialogue ends.	Songs Liturgical Dance Anthem Words of Sending The Benediction Passing the Peace The Postlude

As a planning team we found it helpful to begin with this grid that outlines the pattern for worship. However, we gave ourselves great freedom to decide how each section of the pattern would be composed each week. We have provided a modified form of this grid at the end of the chapter for use by your planning team. There the third column is empty so that you can fill it in as you plan.

A worship planning team will begin its work session with information from the pastor about the Scripture and the sermon for the service. The team then will discuss and formulate the theme of the service, usually to be printed as a sentence at the top of the worship sheet. Each group member should have a worksheet, such as the "Weekly Worship Planning Guide" or "The Pattern of a Worship Service" from the end of this chapter, which they have used for their research and preparation. The team members will usually contribute their suggestions within each movement of the service and often in brainstorming fashion, so all possibilities are offered for discussion. Once suggestions have been offered, the process of making selections will begin. Some items will be eliminated, some modified, and finally agreement will be reached on the elements. Then the elements selected for each section must be ordered in a meaningful way. After this order is constructed, the group should walk through the entire service to be sure there is a flow to this conversation with God. When service planning is completed, someone must take responsibility for communicating instructions to all participants and technicians.

OTHER MATTERS TO KEEP IN MIND

Remember what we've done so far—clarified the purpose and intent, selected Scripture readings, examined our pastoral sensitivity and selected our music—and combined it all into an order of worship. But the team isn't quite finished with its planning. Before the group adjourns, it needs to ask a few other questions.

1. *Does the service have coherence?* No element of worship stands alone. All are interrelated. Worship has sometimes been likened to a choreographed dance. A dance consists of intricate steps, each of which must be mastered, combined, and expressed seamlessly. When you watch a dance, you see a unified flow made up of many

integrated parts. In the same way, worship planning is liturgical choreography. Each element of the worship order must be integrated so that the movement of worship can flow smoothly. Otherwise the result may feel like a potpourri of appealing but disconnected elements. That lack of coherence may not be so noticeable on paper, but it could appear in the actions of Sunday morning. So the liturgy as a whole should be reviewed for cohesiveness. Helpful questions might include:

- Does the service have a theme?
- Are all the elements of this service consistent with this theme?
- Are the spirit and tone of this service compatible with the theme?
- Is there an unbroken progression from the opening to the dismissal?
- Is the music integrated into the liturgy?
- Do the prayers express the theme of the service?
- Are there transitions in the service to move smoothly from one segment to the next?

True, it will take extra time to raise these questions. That's the reason we encourage you to plan early and avoid the last-minute squeeze. The time spent asking these questions will be valuable and will aid in creating an integrated service.

2. *Is it inclusive?* Worshipers are not a uniform group; they represent different ages, experiences, cultures, genders, and backgrounds. For example, some are physically healthy, and some may be disabled. Worshipers bring a wide variety of needs, interests, and personalities. Inclusiveness is therefore as important as coherence.

Making space for a variety of emotions is important. Some seasons will call for vigorous celebrations. Many services need to be marked by hearty praise. But what about other times when the congregation needs to express something different? If worship is to be honest, planners must ask whether they are providing adequate opportunity for worshipers to express their confessions, their pain, their sorrow, and their struggles of faith. Nicholas Wolterstorff, writer and retired professor of philosophy from Yale University, says that worship needs three motifs—"trumpets, ashes, and tears." He observes, "We do not leave behind our experience.... A fundamental dimension of the liturgy is that in it we give expression, in concentrated and condensed ritualized form, precisely to our experience in the world and our response to that experience." (Wolterstorff, "Trumpets, Ashes, and Tears," *Reformed Journal* 36, no. 2 [February 1986], 19). With trumpets we proclaim our vigorous praise and thanks, with ashes we make our confessions before God and seek his grace, and with tears we express our sorrows and laments at the brokenness of life and our world.

We have written earlier about the helpful rhythm of the Christian year to guide our worship planning (see chapter 4). The four weeks of Advent focus on anticipation. Christmas and Epiphany help us celebrate. The six weeks of Lent take us on a journey of self-examination and growth. Easter and Pentecost focus on the power available for the church through the resurrected Christ and the Holy Spirit. Including these various seasonal emphases will likely reach the diversity of people and their needs, as well as various aspects of our relationships with God and neighbor. It will also reenact God's action in salvation history.

3. *Is it balanced in style and form?* Some churches are traditional in the style and forms they use in worship; others plan along a completely contemporary pattern (though we doubt that these terms are helpful since the definition shifts from one person and group to another). The majority of churches today are attempting to balance the historic with the contemporary. Many refer to this as "blended" worship, but we've found that different people also define "blended" differently.

Trying to achieve a balance takes careful work. A planning team should consider the matter thoughtfully and ask probing questions about its efforts to balance the service. Many assume that balancing involves only the songs and music of the worship service. We suggest taking a much broader approach. Aim for a balance between lay and clergy leadership. Some parts of worship should be led by the pastor, but many elements can be led by laypeople. Aim for a mix of all ages so that adults, youth, and children are all included in worship leadership at various times. Aim for a mix of spoken and sung prayers. Let the spoken prayers take various forms—sometimes extemporaneous, sometimes written; recited in unison, or employing spoken or sung responses by the worshipers. Aim for a balance among expressions of praise, thanks, confession, intercession, and lament. Let the songs represent the historic and the contemporary, the local culture and the global church, the expressions of adults and those of children. Worship that is balanced in so many areas can be refreshing and vital.

It is also helpful for worship planners to balance repetition and variety. Repetition makes for security; variety contributes freshness. Most planning teams struggle with the structure of the worship service. Should it follow the same pattern every week? Should it be completely different every week? How much should remain the same and how much should change each week? Worshipers need a sense of familiarity and security, yet overfamiliarity can lull worshipers into inattention. How can we strike a balance?

The structure generally doesn't change, and many of the elements remain the same. But the way even those recurring elements are expressed can change, and lessons, music, sermon, and prayers do change every week. Other elements, such as baptism, communion, confirmation, and other special rites introduce further variety.

Franklin Segler and Randall Bradley write about the model for revitalizing worship design which Brian Wren, hymn writer and professor of worship at Columbia Theological Seminary, Decatur, Georgia, presented at a worship conference at St. Joseph, Missouri. Wren's model involves the weaving together of four patterns:

- *Repetition,* which involves placing the worship elements in the same place and using the same mode of expression each week. Though important for some people, this practice can easily become monotonous.
- *Refreshment,* which involves leaving the elements of worship in the same place but using a different method. This pattern can be a pleasant variation for the sake of freshness.
- *Repositioning,* in which the elements of worship are put in a different place but the same mode of expression is used.
- A combination of *refreshment* and *repositioning* puts worship elements in a different place each time while also using different

methods. This often leaves worshipers struggling to keep up (in Segler and Bradley, *Understanding, Preparing for, and Practicing Christian Worship* [Nashville: Broadman and Holman, 1996], 223-224).

4. *Is it engaging?* One more question must be asked. The worship service that the team puts together is for a public event. That means that putting a service plan on paper is only a preparatory step. The real event will happen on Sunday with real people. Some will come highly motivated and immediately become engaged in worship. Others will have a more difficult time. They are perhaps partially motivated, skeptical, distracted, or just plain uninterested. The goal is to draw them in, and the extent to which we reach this goal rests on how engaging this worship service is. What good will it be if a service is carefully planned but worshipers are not engaged? And what good is the service if worshipers only go through rote motions? In worship we want more than a service on paper, and while the ultimate responsibility for worshiping well rests on each person who comes, the planning team will want to make the service as accessible and engaging as it can to increase the probability of drawing worshipers in.

Much of making worship engaging is influenced by the worship leaders and the way in which they conduct themselves in worship. Disengaged leaders will likely leave many others disengaged. If their spirits are not prepared, they can hardly expect to lead others. But if their enthusiasm and sincerity are transparent, they can inspire others.

Planning team members should examine the service they have planned and ask themselves: Is this likely to attract the worshipers' interest? Does the music at the beginning of the service cause them to anticipate that good things will happen here? Will the call to worship reach the hearts of those present and make them glad to be here? We have found in our experience that the opening three to five minutes of a worship services usually set the tone for much of what follows and determine how engaged many worshipers will be. Sincerity, directness, and sensitivity must be communicated to worshipers during the opening of the service. The opening words of worship should be distinctively Christian to signal that this is a divine-human encounter. Brian Wren has said that the opening of a worship service, especially the music, should send out a "compelling nonverbal signal that *something interesting is happening here!*" (Wren, *Praying Twice* [Louisville: Westminster John Knox, 2000], 381). Such awareness will do much to draw people into this engagement with God. Anthony B. Robinson, senior minister of Plymouth Congregational Church (UCC) of Seattle, quotes the suggestion by Ernest Campbell, onetime pastor of Riverside Church in New York, that instead of trying to plan the extraordinary, we would do well to "energize the ordinary." Robinson goes on to explain that "vivifying" the elements of worship is more important than looking for new bells and whistles to use (Robinson, *Transforming Congregational Culture* [Grand Rapids: Eerdmans, 2003], 52).

So the task of a worship planning team is more complex than we may think. In some traditions, it must create a pattern for the liturgy. All planners must fill in the elements and then prepare it for leaders and print or projection. They should ask the probing questions about their work while they do it, the questions that groups easily avoid. They should ask how much life this crafted pattern will have—Does it show a clear purpose and intent? Are Scripture readings carefully selected? Is there pastoral sensitivity? Has all music been chosen thoughtfully? And then other questions come up when the planners take another look: Is the service cohesive, inclusive, balanced, and engaging? The work of planning worship is not finished until these questions are satisfactorily answered.

SHARED RESOURCES

The work of planning worship requires many resources, and planners who do it week after week often have difficulty finding the resources they need. As musicians need access to a large repertoire of songs, so the planning team needs access to a wide variety of litanies, readings, and prayers. One of the most common questions we encounter is "Where can we find more resources?"

We therefore recommend that each planning team have a library of resources that it shares and freely consults. Resources should include liturgies from previous services, conferences, other churches, journals, and prayer books. These often prove valuable in stirring one's own creativity. Other resources may come from team members' personal libraries. Some may be purchased by the church for their use.

Each team should have access to hymnals or songbooks published by its own denomination or tradition, and several from other denominations and traditions. At least one should be a good children's hymnal. Many of these hymnals provide a leader's edition that contains valuable information about songs and how to use them. Planners should become familiar with and know how to use the indexes. Most hymnals have Scripture indexes that pair hymn texts with Scripture passages; most also include a metrical index that allows worship planners to pair hymn texts with alternate tunes. In addition, many denominational hymnals provide a concordance that enables planners to search for a hymn text that matches a word or theme. The planning team will want to have resources in each of the categories below. This list is not intended to be complete, but it offers a beginning for each team to build on.

Denominational Hymnals

Anglican Church of Canada, *Common Praise*
Christian Church (Disciples of Christ), *Chalice Hymnal*
Christian Reformed Church, *Psalter Hymnal*
Church of the Brethren, General Conference Mennonite Churches, and Mennonite Churches of North America, *Hymnal: A Worship Book*
Episcopal Church, *The Hymnal 1982*
Evangelical Lutheran Church in America, *Lutheran Book of Worship*
Lutheran Church–Missouri Synod, *Lutheran Worship*
Mennonite Brethren, *Worship Together*
Moravian Church in America, *Moravian Book of Worship*
Presbyterian Church (U.S.A.), *Presbyterian Hymnal*
Presbyterian Church in Canada, *The Book of Praise*
Presbyterian Church of America/Orthodox Presbyterian Church, *Trinity Hymnal*
Reformed Church in American, *Rejoice in the Lord*
Roman Catholic, *Lead Me Guide Me, Gather, Gather Comprehensive, RitualSong, Glory and Praise, We Celebrate, Catholic Community*

Hymnal, Worship III
Southern Baptist Convention, *The Baptist Hymnal*
United Church of Canada, *Voices United*
United Church of Christ, *New Century Hymnal*
United Methodist Church, *The United Methodist Hymnal*
Wisconsin Evangelical Lutheran Synod, *Christian Worship*

Supplementary Hymnals

African American Heritage Hymnal, GIA
The Faith We Sing, Abingdon
Hymnal Supplement 98, Concordia Publishing House
Hymns for the Gospels, GIA
Lift Every Voice and Sing II, Church Hymnal Corporation
Lift Up Your Hearts, Geneva Press
One Is the Body: Songs of Unity and Diversity; Wee Worship Book; Many and Great; Sent by the Lord; Come All You People: Shorter Songs for Worship; Songs from Iona Community, GIA
Psalms for Praise and Worship, Abingdon
Renew! Hope Publishing Company
Sing! A New Creation, from Calvin Institute of Christian Worship, the Christian Reformed Church, and the Reformed Church in America, Faith Alive Christian Resources
Songs from Taizé; Songs for Prayer; Songs and Prayers from Taizé, from Taizé Community (France), GIA
Songs of Zion, Abingdon
This Far by Faith, Augsburg Fortress
With One Voice, Augsburg Fortress
Wonder, Love, and Praise, Church Publishing Incorporated
Worship & Rejoice, Hope Publishing Company
The Worshiping Church, Hope Publishing Company

Children's Hymnals

All God's People Sing, Concordia Publishing House
LifeSongs, Augsburg Fortress
Rise Up and Sing: Young People's Music Resource, OCP Publications
Songs for LiFE, a children's songbook, Faith Alive Christian Resources.

To God With Love, Selah Publishing Co.
We Sing of God, The Church Hymnal Corporation

Liturgical Resources

The Book of Common Prayer, Oxford University Press
The Book of Common Worship, Westminster John Knox Press
The Chorister, a journal of the Choristers Guild
The Lutheran Book of Worship, Augsburg Publishing House and Board of
    Publication, Lutheran Church in America
The New Handbook of the Christian Year, Abingdon
Occasional Book of Services: A Companion to the Lutheran Book of Worship,
    Augsburg Publishing House and Board of Publication, Lutheran Church
    in America
Plan a Worship Service, Faith Alive Christian Resources
The Revised Common Lectionary, The Consultation on Common Texts
Reformed Worship, a quarterly journal published by Faith Alive Christian
    Resources,
The Sourcebook of Worship Resources, (vols. 1 and 2), Communication
    Resources, Inc.
Ten Service Plans for Contemporary Worship, CRC Publications
Worship Planning Calendar, Augsburg Fortress
The Worship Sourcebook, Calvin Institute of Christian Worship, Faith Alive
    Christian Resources, Baker Book House

General Studies in Worship

The list of resources at the end of this book provides many such resources.
Planning teams will benefit from engaging in a group study of the issues of
worship.

DRAWING IT TOGETHER

Those who come to worship on Sunday will not be aware of all the work the
planning team has contributed. They will not know the hours of research
and planning, the prayers, the writing and rewriting, the discussions and
questions, and all the editing. And that's as it should be. This is intended to

be strategic but invisible work. Only the fruit of this work shows up in public.

But when this team works together well, collaborating in a healthy manner and creating a worship service that is vital and engaging, when it is thoughtful enough to ask probing questions about its work, then that congregation will be a rich and rewarding place to worship. People will be drawn into the presence of God. Lives will be changed. God will be honored and pleased. And the community of faith will be encouraged and enriched.

WEEKLY WORSHIP PLANNING GUIDE (SAMPLE)

Each member of the planning team should have a copy of the worksheet [on the following page] *for each service to be planned. It is to be used for their preparation work before the meeting. All team members should complete the items in their area of responsibility.*

Weekly Worship Planning Guide

Date: _____ AM ___ PM ___

Season of the Christian Year: _____

Theme of the Service: _____

Sacrament: _____

Special Events: _____

Preacher: _____

Sermon Title: _____

Sermon Scripture: _____

Series of Sermons: _____

Supplemental Scripture Readings: _____

Confessional or Catechism Reference: _____

Organist/Pianist: _____

Other Musicians: _____

Anthems/Ministry of Music

    Title and composer: _____

    Participants: _____

Possible Congregational Songs

    Psalms: _____

    Other Scripture Songs: _____

    Children's Hymns: _____

    Hymns: _____

    Descants: _____

Prelude: _____

Offertory: _____

Postlude: _____

Children's Message

    Theme: _____

    Leader: _____

Lay Liturgists

    Scripture Readings: _____

    Prayers: _____

    Other: _____

Liturgical Dance: _____

THE PATTERN OF A WORSHIP SERVICE (SAMPLE)

Consult the completed copy of this grid [see page 134]. Note the possible elements cited. Use this as a worksheet for worship planning by determining the elements in the third column and ordering them.

The Pattern of Worship

Movement	Purpose	Possible Elements
The Gathering	The corporate conversation between God and his children is begun. God's children are entering his presence and the dialogue begins.	1. 2. 3. 4. 5. 6.
The Renewal	As worshipers come into the presence of a holy God, they acknowledge their sinfulness and seek forgiveness and renewal in God's grace.	1. 2. 3. 4. 5. 6.
The Word	God's Word is proclaimed, so that his voice is heard and his people are instructed and strengthened.	1. 2. 3. 4.
The Response to God's Word	God's Word always calls for a response on the part of those who hear. This section provides opportunities for responses of faith, thanksgiving, and obedience.	1. 2. 3. 4. 5. 6.
The Lord's Supper	A major response of God's people to his Word is our participation in the body and blood of our Lord.	1. 2. 3. 4.
The Dismissal	The corporate conversation between God and his people comes to an end, and elements are provided by which we take leave of each other. The dialogue ends.	1. 2. 3. 4. 5. 6.

CHAPTER 6

WORSHIP EVALUATION

In a few months, the Lenten season would begin. Karen and Mario were starting their Lenten planning. Each had formulated some ideas. Karen was working on a series of sermons. Mario had gathered a stack of potential anthems and a list of possible hymns. Their planning time to chart out the season was scheduled for Tuesday afternoon, and both were eager. As they began their planning session, both had a paper in hand titled "Lenten Review Sheet." This compilation of the comments from the worship committee's review of Lenten worship last year was a gold mine of ideas and reflections, the kinds of things they might easily have forgotten. The review sheet, which included the special events of the previous year, reminded them of what had been most beneficial in shaping the congregation's worship, and what had not served particularly well and needed revision. This review also included many of the logistical and mechanical details that had been part of last year's planning—how many palm branches were ordered for the children for Palm Sunday, the lighting arrangements for Good Friday, and a host of other matters. The review sheet included both an assessment of how the service had gone and what changes might be needed in the future.

Last night the worship committee of Crestview Church held its monthly meeting. At each meeting members spend a short time reviewing and evaluating the worship services of the past month. Sometimes this discussion is open and helpful; sometimes it seems that none of the members has much to say. Last night was one of those nights when little was said. That was frustrating to Stan and Ina. As preaching pastor and minister of music, respectively, they were eager for feedback on the worship services. But what bothered them even more was seeing several of the committee members standing by their cars in the parking lot after the meeting engaged in animated conversation. What were they talking about? Did they have more to say out there than they did in the meeting? Were they telling each other of criticisms they'd heard about the services that they didn't dare share in the meeting? Those questions haunted Stan and Ina.

Mondays are often slow for Jorge. On Sunday he has poured himself out in leading worship and preaching. He is weary in body and spirit. At such times he tends to be easily discouraged, reminding himself how he could have improved his sermon and presented it more effectively. His wife, Viviana, tries to encourage him, but it's always a struggle for Jorge to get through Monday, given his tendency to second-guess himself. He wonders if he is the only pastor who does that. But this Monday was different. He went to the office to sort through the mail, do some filing, and get ready for the week, and to his surprise he found a couple of e-mail messages waiting for him. With some curiosity he opened them to discover that Sue had made the effort to tell him she found yesterday's prayer particularly meaningful. She'd been dealing with a lot of stress in her family lately, and the way Jorge led in prayer expressed her thoughts in a way she wasn't able to do herself. "I want you to know, Pastor, that you put me right in God's lap in that prayer!" she wrote. The second was from a senior member of the congregation who told Jorge that the message on Romans 8 had given him comfort and assurance. "Sometimes people forget that those of us who are older need our hearts encouraged and our faith propped up! You did that, Pastor! Thanks!" Jorge smiled. The week seemed much more attractive to him now.

The subject of worship evaluation feels new to most worship planners. Surely evaluations have always been done, but they've usually happened in the parking lot or over coffee in private homes. Seldom have they been done in a formal, structured, and wholesome manner. But given the process of worship renewal taking place in churches today, the practice of regular evaluation is becoming more common.

It's easy for worship planners and leaders to feel somewhat insecure and threatened by an evaluation of worship. When we hear "evaluation" we wince, associating it with "report card" or some other unpleasant memory. After all, we put so much of ourselves and our souls into a worship service that when comments about the worship are made, we feel they are directed at us. Because we personalize our work, we tend to feel that such assessments reflect on our personal worth. While we know evaluations are done privately every week by many folk, we are not ordinarily subjected to them directly. We're often just too fragile to handle such criticism objectively.

Yet at the same time, we need to hear what went well, how we have blessed people, and what was appreciated. Yes, it's often devastating to hear sharp criticism, but it's most encouraging to receive appreciation.

In consulting with other worship planners, we have discovered that while most churches do little if any formal worship evaluation, those who plan feel uncomfortable about that lack. These planners sense that they ought to be evaluating in some way but aren't quite sure how, or how to get started. This chapter is written for those who have that concern. We want to encourage churches to develop a thoughtful, faithful, and fair feedback process that will provide encouragement and growth for both their leaders and their members.

APPRAISALS AS CHRISTIAN PRACTICE

Worship evaluation will make more sense if we see it in a broad context. All good athletes are constantly evaluating their performance and searching for ways to improve. They read, check out videos, and search for coaches and teachers who can help them see and feel what they are doing and guide them in how to do it better. Artists of all sorts do the same to draw out of themselves the highest skills. Those in the business world also frequently participate in performance reviews. The art of evaluation and appraisal is an essential ingredient in so much human activity.

It can also be said that appraisal should be a distinctively Christian practice. Craig Dykstra, vice president for religion at Lilly Endowment, Inc., said, "It makes a lot of sense for us to be asking ourselves all the way along whether what we are doing is really making that difference, whether we really are doing it as well as it can be done, and whether we are in fact spending our selves and our resources on what really matters." Dykstra put this idea in the context of Christian practice: "I suspect that behind virtually every endeavor undertaken by a religious organization there lies a hope that the new thing we do—or the ongoing thing we keep on doing—will, in one way or another, be an expression and embodiment of a fitting response to the call we hear to love God and our neighbors" (in Kathleen A. Calahan, *Projects That Matter: Successful Planning and Evaluation for Religious Organizations* [Bethesda: Alban Institute, 2003], vii–viii).

The Christian church should foster a culture in which a variety of appraisals are welcomed and encouraged, and where members have learned how to evaluate constructively and lovingly. We've seen churches in which a rancid and unbridled atmosphere of negative criticism has been harmful and destructive. But we've also seen churches in which evaluation has been commonly accepted and surrounded with loving commitments to promote growth in one another for the sake of more effective ministry. Such churches show their love for God and one another.

These Christian appraisals include several types of evaluation. First is *ministry evaluation.* Groups responsible for each of the ministries of the church will periodically ask themselves probing questions about their ministry. "What are we doing that promotes healthy ministry here? What strengths have we illustrated in the past year? What causes for concern should we address?"

The second area of appraisal efforts includes *staff evaluations.* Staff members should welcome periodic appraisals of their work so they can learn what areas of their work are most effective and in what areas they need additional growth and training. It is vital that these appraisals be conducted confidentially and in a spirit of trust and love. They must also be conducted by a trusted committee that is responsible for the supervision of staff. In some traditions this practice is commonplace; in others not. In a recent survey by the National Opinion Research Center, clergy were asked, "Do you and your leaders engage in an annual evaluation of your performance?" Of 900 survey respondents, 58 percent said they have an annual performance evaluation. Mainline Protestant clergy reported the highest incidence at 79 percent. Roman Catholic clergy were the lowest at 32 percent. African American clergy were slightly above that at 34 percent. And conservative evangelical Protestant clergy were in the middle at 46 percent (*Congregations,* vol. 28, no. 2, published by Alban Institute, March/April 2002, 6).

A third and more specific area for appraisal includes *sermon evaluation*. Many pastors feel rather uncertain about participating in this process, but when evaluation is done well it can be a source of immense help and encouragement. The preacher should engage in his or her own appraisals by watching videos or listening to tapes of sermons and services. Asking such questions as "How do I lead?" can open the door to learning. Watching gestures and posture, listening to words, noting eye contact and facial expressions—all these can give the preacher new insights. It is also helpful to analyze the flow of thought, the clarity of ideas, and the persuasiveness of the sermon. It can be difficult to evaluate ourselves objectively, but we often get a much different view of ourselves and our sermons when we watch or listen to them later. We become aware of potential improvements that beg to be made. In addition, the preacher will benefit from the insights and feedback given by trusted church leaders. The evaluation should focus on whether the sermons are faithful to God's Word, appropriate to the needs of the listeners, and presented in a compelling way. The wise preacher will draw on the insights of wise leaders to learn what needs of the congregation and community ought to be addressed in future preaching. The situational analysis form at the end of this chapter has often been used profitably as the preacher searches for insight in planning sermons.

Similarly, musicians should engage in a *music evaluation* of themselves and their leadership. They should, for example, be asking whether they set good and steady tempos for congregational singing, whether they allow adequate time for the congregation to breathe between hymn phrases, whether they select hymns and anthems consistent with the theme of the service and representative of a range of musical traditions. These probing questions will open the door to better understanding and development.

THE CASE FOR WORSHIP EVALUATION

A church whose culture welcomes appraisals as part of its ongoing work and whose members have learned to do so positively and constructively will also be a community that can welcome worship evaluations. While this may indeed be a new effort in some communities, great benefits can be gained from it. Something as valuable and integral to the total life of a congregation as its worship merits close evaluation and attention.

Here are some of the key benefits for congregations that learn to evaluate their worship well.

1. *Those who serve well will receive encouragement.* Most of us who serve tend to be hard on ourselves. We second-guess ourselves, think afterward of ways in which we wish we had led differently, and sometimes exaggerate our mistakes. Most of the time we wonder if anyone else appreciates our efforts. Sure, we all have to struggle with our motives for leading—are we doing it for God's glory and the benefit of others, or to receive the approval of others?—but the fact remains that those who lead publicly need encouragement to carry on in such a risky venture. So we wonder if others were blessed by our leadership. How rich it is to have someone say "thank you, well done!" How healthy it is to affirm those new to leading worship and how encouraging to receive reviews that our efforts contributed to the health of our congregation's worship life!

2. *Evaluation will balance out negative criticism so easily made.* Those who lead in public events must always live with negative criticism. Complaints do come. And it seems that they come so easily. Sometimes we receive them directly, and we at least have an opportunity to discuss the matter. But more often we receive them indirectly, and those who criticize remain unidentified phantoms. Most of us are stung by negative criticism when we sense that it is not offered in a constructive spirit. Yet certain church folk thrive on offering it. A structured and thoughtful system of feedback by informed individuals can balance out the negative criticism we may hear directly or second- or thirdhand.

3. *Evaluation can stir our creativity and motivation.* We are able to step outside our personal frame of reference and look at a worship service from others' experiences as evaluations are made. People who speak the truth from their heart will bless us by allowing us to view the worship through their eyes, and thus to stretch and grow in our ability to lead well. The creative energy that we need for vital worship planning will increase as we receive this feedback from others.

4. *Evaluation will enhance seasonal worship planning.* When Karen and Mario at the opening of this chapter began their seasonal planning for Lent, they found it helpful to have a review sheet from the

Benefits of Worship Evaluation

1. Those who serve well will receive encouragement.
2. Evaluation will balance out negative criticism easily made.
3. Evaluation can fuel and stir our creativity and motivation.
4. Evaluation will enhance seasonal planning.
5. Evaluation provides a healthy corrective in our planning.
6. Evaluation will encourage the development of thoughtful and wise practices.
7. Evaluation reminds us that our work is not about us.
8. Intentional evaluation can provide a safeguard.

previous year. Each year they could learn from the year before, prompting an annual growth process. Worship planners who save bulletins and make comments on them will find them highly valuable for future planning. The files of last year with all their evaluative comments can become the starting point for planning the coming year. Many of the comments from last year would be forgotten if not for the written review, and learning opportunities would be squandered.

5. *Evaluation provides a healthy corrective in our planning.* Subtle influences, many of which we are unaware, shape our worship planning. It's easy to get off track and lose focus. We may find that the direction of our worship shifts slightly and gradually. Not until later do we see that the accumulated slight shifts made large differences. A healthy evaluation process will catch the shifts and enable us to make necessary corrections. Evaluation is a good safeguard.

6. *Evaluation will encourage the development of thoughtful and wise practices.* We need corrections from unhealthy shifts, but we also need to have our healthy practices reinforced until they are ingrained habits. When we know the spiritual impact of certain worship practices and make a note to ourselves, "Be sure to do this again," we will reinforce good habits. When we learn what proves to be distracting and resolve not to try it again, we will develop wise practices. So all evaluations have "for next time" written all over them. "Next time" will serve better because we've evaluated "this time."

7. *Evaluation reminds us that our work is not about us.* Evaluations also provide times for the humbling of egos. Though that hurts, it's not bad. Our work in worship planning is not for us or for our credit, but to aid this gathering of God's people in his presence to engage in dialogue with him. If it were only about us, evaluations might not be necessary. But since our efforts are part of such a large cause, and since the purpose is found far beyond ourselves, the evaluation provides us with the constant reminder that our efforts are not for ourselves but for God and others.

8. *Intentional evaluation can provide a safeguard against hyper-evaluation.* Sometimes too much evaluation can be done. When it is intentional and structured, we are protected from this excess. The best and most profitable evaluations are done at the right time and in the right setting. Too much too soon can be harmful to both the planner and the evaluation process.

In all such efforts, we should remember that the purpose is not to grade or score each other or ourselves, but to gain better insight into what we are doing and to find ways to improve it.

CRITERIA FOR EVALUATIONS

Evaluations can be helpful or damaging. Sometimes the spirit in which they are offered determines that, but more often the criteria used become the determining factor. Suppose we're going to evaluate the Sunday morning service. One person judges it on the basis of the percentage of songs in his preferred style; another evaluates it by how traditional the liturgy was; and the third evaluates it with an eye to the musical instruments used. All will come with different evaluations. The risk is clear. If each evaluator comes with a personal set of values, the evaluations will not be very helpful. Evaluations, therefore, are best done by a group of participants who have agreed on a set of values that will serve as the criteria.

Several dangers need to be avoided. Evaluators must avoid the "personal taste or preference" issues. Evaluations that begin with "I like . . ." or "I just don't like . . ." are usually not helpful. And evaluations that focus on style issues prove to be divisive because each evaluator runs the service through the grid of his or her preferred worship style. Similarly, evaluators must not see worship as a personal performance of the worship leaders or they'll tend to evaluate it as public performance. Because we live and worship in a consumer-oriented culture in which so many things are market-driven, it is helpful to remind ourselves that worship should not be evaluated on the basis of its market appeal to the consumer of worship. If the market provides the criteria, we will easily focus on secondary matters and avoid the deeper issues of worship. A wise evaluator will also try to rise above matters of mechanics and logistics. While it may be important where the praise team stood, or if the microphones were too conspicuous, or if there was too much moving around, and so on, those concerns are secondary to the intent of the service. The best evaluations will drive down to the deeper questions and issues of the essence of worship. So a group of evaluators must lay aside such secondary criteria.

So what criteria ought to be used? What kinds of questions should we ask? And of those, which are fundamental? So often evaluations focus on the mechanics of the service—the way things happened. Or they focus on the style—did it reflect the needs and desires of our congregation? But the most valuable evaluations will deal with more substantial matters such as the integration and flow of the service—did it follow a coherent theme? And then we must focus on the deepest question of all about the essence of worship—were we helped in our praying and meeting God?

Levels of Criteria for Evaluation

1. The mechanics of the service
2. The style of worship
3. The flow of the liturgy
4. The essence of worship

In an effort to understand the importance of our criteria, we ought to listen to a few people who have distinguished themselves as clear thinkers on worship issues. They help us rise above the secondary evaluative questions and engage us in the primary questions.

Anthony Robinson, in *Transforming Congregational Culture* (Grand Rapids: Eerdmans, 83) tells of a colleague who suggests three brief but useful questions to guide our reflection on all ministry, and certainly on worship: "What did I give? What did I receive? Where did I encounter God?"

These questions prod us to think of the two sides of worship—both giving and receiving.

Marva Dawn, who writes on worship issues, pleads with us to ask the biggest questions possible about worship. In *How Shall We Worship? Biblical Guidelines for Worship Wars* (Wheaton, Ill.: Tyndale House, 2003, 138), she encourages us to ask questions such as these:

> Do we, over the course of time, include enough Scriptures so that we expose worship participants to "the whole counsel of God"? Do our worship services fill participants with such joy in God's sovereignty that they eagerly tell their neighbors about God's reign? Is the picture of God in worship so comprehensive that the saints are equipped to live the rest of the week as missional people?

In other words, "When we leave the worship service has our character been nurtured by visions of God's reign so that we will be agents of Triune righteousness and faithfulness in the world—God's purposes to feed the hungry, combat oppressions, expose the lies, live the truth?" (152).

Then Dawn recommends that we use questions like these in a group exercise. You can find her more complete explanations of each of the following queries in *A Royal "Waste" of Time* (Grand Rapids: Eerdmans, 1999, 302-313).

1. What is appropriate for displaying the character and interventions of God?
2. Are these lines appropriately written?
3. Is this music appropriately written?
4. Are music and text appropriately coherent?
5. What is appropriate for forming the character of the followers of Christ?
6. What is appropriate for developing a sense of the Church catholic?
7. What is appropriate for building community in this place?
8. What is appropriate for the level of the congregation's ability to participate?
9. What is appropriate for including more of the gifts of the people in the worship space and time?
10. What is appropriate for envisioning the reign of God with all its truth, beauty, and goodness?

11. What is appropriate to create a missional community?
12. What is appropriate for the level of pain in the world?
13. What is appropriate for this time in the Church year?
14. What is appropriate for the texts of the day?
15. What is appropriate for this place in the worship service?
16. What is appropriate to evoke the recognition that we need more, to create a hunger and thirst for worship again next week?

Paul Basden, pastor of Brookwood Baptist Church in Birmingham, Alabama, suggests these questions to cover both the content and the impact of worship (Basden, *The Worship Maze: Finding a Style to Fit Your Church* [Downers Grove, Ill.: InterVarsity Press, 1999], 145).

1. Were the facilities and equipment ready? (sound system, lights, air conditioning and so on).
2. Were the worship leaders fully notified and prepared? (laity and ministers).
3. Did key lay leaders make any significant comments about the service?
4. Did each element of worship meet its goal?
5. Did the "laos" (the people of God) actively participate in worship?
6. Did the service have an identifiable flow and direction?
7. Were God's transcendence and immanence portrayed?
8. Did people leave the service aware of God's love, grace, and power?
9. Did people leave knowing that their sins were forgiven?
10. Did people encounter God in a life-changing way?

Questions such as these shape the evaluations forms we've included at the end of the chapter (see page 169). You are free to use these in any way you find helpful. We recommend that such evaluations be conducted through group discussions.

We should also watch worshipers' nonverbal expressions. Worship leaders must develop the ability to read such cues. Some responses are experienced on too deep a level to put into words, so worship leaders with a pastoral sense will watch and listen for messages that come from the eyes and facial expressions of worshipers as they listen, the vigor of the singing, the noise level or restlessness within the congregation, and the apparent degree of attentiveness. Leading worship at a church where the lighting makes it difficult to read such signals puts a worship leader at a severe disadvantage. It's helpful to chat with people in the narthex after the service. When the pastor greets worshipers he or she will often sense the level of their response. Whenever Herm was touched by something in a worship service, he met the pastor at the door and held the pastor's hand in both his hands—with no words. Tears in the eye or a simple emotional "thanks" will often speak volumes. Worship leaders also learn to listen to notes written later in the week, and for comments made days afterwards that point to a lingering impact.

AN EVALUATION PLAN

Each congregation needs to develop a plan for worship evaluation that suits its own needs and structure. Such a plan will likely include multiple levels of evaluation. Various groups will be involved. Frequency will vary. So will the thoroughness of the evaluations. Before explaining the levels, we want to caution that congregation-wide worship surveys usually do not provide a great deal of helpful material. Such surveys can easily politicize the process and leave the impression that worship is planned on the basis of popular preference. No standard criteria can be assured. It is usually better for worship planners and worship committee members to keep their ears attuned for comments from members of the congregation. One musician/worship planner solicits comments from key members of the congregation as a valued part of her self-evaluation. These members know what the mission of the congregation is, have a good understanding of what worship is, and will make thoughtful comments about the services. We all need extra sets of ears! We must, of course, not surround ourselves only with those who will tell us what we want to hear, but to seek out those who will be thoughtful and faithful. We must learn to be gracious in such conversations and to accept both thanks and criticism with the same spirit.

Post-Worship Debriefing

Before talking about the more formal evaluations, we note the need for some immediate post-service critique. But first we raise some cautions. In some instances this kind of debriefing may not be helpful. Perhaps it could make you so self-aware in worship that you would not worship well. Perhaps your worship experience has been so deep that it would be tarnished by examining it immediately. Or perhaps you're upset or disappointed that things didn't go well and you need to let your emotions settle a couple of days before you can discuss it thoughtfully and objectively. In addition, perhaps you are fragile and need a few days before critiquing the worship.

Having said that, we still believe that it is often wise and helpful for most to linger a short while and exchange some ideas before leaving for home. The conversations in the narthex have been valuable, and now most of the folk have left. So the major worship leaders or planners can put their ideas together for a few minutes before leaving. True, this approach carries risks because these comments can be subjective. Worship leaders are hardly in a position to be objective in the first half-hour after worship! Yet there may be significant impressions—thoughts that might be lost 48 hours from now. These 10 minutes of preliminary debriefing are informal and usually positive, unless some glaring weakness stood out and must be noted. The conversation usually centers on such questions as: "What went well?" "What could have gone better?" "What was the overall spirit of the worshipers at the close of the service?" The participants draw on any comments or conversations they have had with others in the narthex. Because this evaluation is so brief and subjective, it can only be the first step. A formal group evaluation can complete the process with greater objectivity.

Worship Planning Team Evaluations

Balanced worship evaluations will need to be a group effort. Multiple eyes and ears will provide broad insight and observations. When a larger number of people work with an agreed upon set of criteria, they can provide a high-quality evaluation. All contribute from their own perspective and provide a more complete picture. Such group evaluations are a collaborative inquiry with a common commitment to grow.

Peter Steinke, a Lutheran pastor and a church consultant, captures the danger of isolated, individual evaluations in the story about the six blind men who encounter an elephant. Each of the sightless men evaluates the elephant from his own perspective:

Six wise men of India
An elephant did find
And carefully they felt its shape
(For all of them were blind).

The first he felt towards the tusk,
"It does to me appear,
This marvel of an elephant
Is very like a spear."

The second sensed the creature's side
Extended flat and tall,
"Ahah!" he cried and did conclude,
"This animal's a wall."

The third had reached toward a leg
And said, "It's clear to me
What we should all have instead
This creature's like a tree."

The fourth had come upon the trunk
Which he did seize, and shake,
Quoth he, "This so-called elephant
Is really just a snake."

The fifth had felt the creature's ear
And finger o'er it ran,
"I have the answer, never fear,
The creature's like a fan!"

The sixth had come upon the tail
As blindly he did grope,
"Let my conviction now prevail
This creature's like a rope."

And so these men of missing sight
Each argued loud and long
Though each was partly in the right
They all were in the wrong.

[Peter Steinke, *Healthy Congregations: A Systems Approach* (Bethesda: Alban Institute, 1996). Apparently based on a verse by John Godfrey Saxe (1816-1881), from his "Poems" (Boston, 1852).]

The worship planning team is the first group that enters the scene for evaluations. Since this group meets weekly, the most regular and intensive worship evaluation can be done here. Before this planning group begins planning services, time should be taken to review the services of the previous Sunday. Many find that memories can be unreliable, and it's best to have a copy of the order of worship with comments that were written in last Sunday. To critique the service without the order of worship in hand allows the evaluation to wander in generalities. Some groups will have an evaluation form to guide them, similar to those at the end of this chapter. Others will come with their own set of questions. One worship planner always comes with this checklist:

1. Were the selections of texts for readings, songs, and so on appropriate?
2. Were the various elements of the service integrated and coordinated into wholesome worship?
3. Did we communicate well with each other in our preparation and leading?
4. Were the readings and music well prepared?
5. Did technology aid or distract? (sound, lights, projections, and so on).
6. What suggestions do you have for future planning?

Since the members of the worship planning team are directly involved in worship planning and leading on a week-to-week basis, they are able to engage in an ongoing evaluation of the worship life of the church. Sometimes they will find it difficult to be objective because the service they are evaluating is one that they planned, but one would hope that the level of trust within the group will enable members to overcome this potential hindrance. As they engage in weekly evaluations, they will discover that evaluating the worship of the past week greatly assists them in planning for the next week.

Some groups find the convenience of e-mail a great aid in their evaluation process. Even before the planning team meets, the members have been exchanging e-mail reflections with each other. Loop Christian Ministries in Chicago relies on weekly evaluative e-mail messages. The chairperson usually starts the e-mail exchange the day after the service, beginning with something positive about the service (always a good thing to do!) and including something that needs improvement. This message is sent to all planning team members, and all are invited to respond. This exchange of ideas before the group's next face-to-face meeting forms the basis for additional comments and evaluations at the meeting.

Worship Committee Evaluations

Chapter 2 described the difference between the worship planning team and the worship committee. Whereas the planning team meets weekly for the hands-on work of planning, the worship committee ordinarily meets monthly to consider policy decisions and longer-range matters, and may engage in some brainstorming on worship planning. The worship committee therefore will likely have a greater degree of objectivity in its evaluation efforts. The membership will usually reflect a broader range of the congregation than the planning team does, but because this group meets monthly at most, more time will pass before evaluations take place. Details of particular services may well have faded from memory, yet their overall assessment can provide a healthy supplement to the planning team evaluations.

In some committees, the agenda for each month includes a regular time for evaluation, though it will be more cursory since multiple services are in view. We recommend giving copies of orders of worship to committee members to refresh their memories of the services they are evaluating. In our experience, the evaluation section of the agenda would highlight a few key services of the past month with some key questions to direct the discussion at the meeting. You may not feel the need to evaluate services every month. Perhaps quarterly or seasonally is sufficient—particularly if you have not engaged in evaluation in the past.

Here are a few scenarios for committee evaluation that we've experienced. The agenda for one of the meetings included a line item like this:

During the past month we've had some highly intensive worship times—Taizé-style worship, Palm Sunday, Good Friday, and Easter. Join us in reflecting on them.

1. Cite several things that stand out as especially helpful in your encounter with God.
2. Cite a few comments from others that will give us an indication of what others experienced during these services.

3. Point to a couple of items that didn't quite measure up to what you think they should have been, and suggest how they could have been improved.

At other times a seasonal block of worship services would be in view, and the committee would have an opportunity to review a series of services. At the conclusion of Lent, it was helpful to review the entire season and see it as a whole. Committee members could point to elements that stood out as particularly devotional, songs that carried the spirit of the season exceptionally well, and areas in which the services could have been improved. The same is true for any other season of the Christian year.

A topical series of sermons provides another occasion for evaluation. If the pastor has presented six sermons on "The Hard Questions of the Christian Life," the committee should comment on questions such as:

- Was it a good series for the congregation?
- Did worshipers find help and encouragement?
- Were the worship services and the sermon integrated so that each reinforced the other?
- Can you give examples of where and when that happened?

Remember that these evaluations done by the worship committee should be seen as supplements to weekly evaluations by the planning team; they serve as a check and balance for each other. Remember also two other considerations to this healthy process. First, the development of trusting and honest relationships within the group is a necessary prerequisite for high-quality evaluation sessions. And second, it is essential to make appointments to the committee prayerfully and wisely. The membership must reflect the age and gender of the congregation, but the members must also be people who have good relationships with others in the congregation, who are themselves trusted, and who are able to listen well.

Church Board Evaluations

In all congregations a board is ultimately responsible for the supervision of the church and its ministries. The board members may be called trustees, deacons, elders, or carry some other title. The worship committee and worship planning team will have received their mandate from this board.

Though the church board usually cannot and should not be involved in the week-to-week work of planning and evaluating worship, neither should it wash its hands of this responsibility. From time to time the board should be encouraged to do its own evaluation of the congregation's worship life. Since some representatives of the worship committee will likely be on this board, good communication can flow between the two groups.

Annually, or perhaps semi-annually, the board can benefit from stepping away from its regular agenda for an overall evaluation of the congregation's worship life. Members of the worship committee may be invited to join the effort, or the worship committee may be invited to present a report on its view of things as preparation for this exercise. You may select one of the evaluation forms provided at the end of the chapter to use as a tool to "prime the pump" for this discussion. Some church boards may desire to organize a few "focus groups"—small groups of eight to 12 members of the congregation, in which they can solicit the viewpoints of other worshipers.

EVALUATIONS FOR GROWTH

While many of us may find that the idea of evaluations produces anxiety, sending us back to those days when we brought a report card home, there is a better way of looking at it. We grow when we are given the gift of constructive evaluations. Midcourse corrections, usually necessary, can be made only when we stop to take a discerning look. The worship of the church becomes more vital when its leaders and planners are able to benefit from the thoughtful insights of others. It is essential, however, that no worship leader be made to feel like an object to be graded by others. We all are engaged in a God-honoring ministry that we desire constantly to improve for the honor of God and the benefit of those who participate.

In all our evaluations we must discern the fine line between being faithful and offering God our very best, yet not feeling the pressure to be perfect. We honor the efforts of those who give their best and always encourage them. At the same time, we want to foster growth and deepening in Christian service and never discourage anyone whose contribution is not yet perfect.

When we asked a group of worship planners to identify the most satisfying part of their work, one said, "In all our work grace abounds!" So may yours!

SITUATIONAL ANALYSIS FORM

As someone actively involved in the life of this congregation, you have received impressions and information that provide you with a knowledge of the personal needs of its members. You may have received that knowledge in any of several ways—personal conversations, pastoral calling, family visitation, group interactions, and so on.

You will provide vital assistance in the planning of preaching by indicating the matters that you believe preaching must address during the coming year. Be sure that you make your selection below on the basis of what you believe the congregation needs and not just on your personal preference.

A. Questions of faith (Please check the three most important ones):

- ☐ the assurance of salvation
- ☐ discernment of God's will for our lives
- ☐ the need for personal conversion
- ☐ matters of eschatology and the "last things"
- ☐ the practice of stewardship (of finances, time resources, creation)
- ☐ the life of worship
- ☐ the practice of sharing our faith
- ☐ Christian education for children and youth

B. Matters of doctrine (Please check the three most important ones):

- ☐ salvation by the grace of God alone
- ☐ the person and work of Christ
- ☐ the nature and task of the Christian church
- ☐ the work and power of the Holy Spirit
- ☐ sin and repentance
- ☐ the creation and providence of God
- ☐ the inspiration and authority of Scripture
- ☐ the greatness and sovereignty of God

C. Personal Growth (Please check the three most important ones):

- ☐ preparing for and maintaining Christian marriages
- ☐ being Christian parents
- ☐ growing through affliction and suffering

☐ living with an unforgiving spirit

☐ overcoming the tendency to be complacent

☐ overcoming fear and anxiety

☐ discovering and developing spiritual gifts

☐ establishing and maintaining better personal relationships

D. Moral/Ethical Issues (Please check the three most important ones):

☐ the sacredness of life

☐ matters of abuse (physical, emotional, verbal, and sexual)

☐ materialism

☐ divorce and remarriage

☐ racism, prejudice, and injustice

☐ poverty and world hunger

☐ war and world peace

☐ the relationships of church and state

E. Temptations (Please check the three most important ones):

☐ greed, envy, and jealousy

☐ lust and adultery

☐ a critical spirit toward others

☐ a spirit of self-centeredness

☐ hedonism and the pleasure-filled life

☐ Sabbath practices

☐ dishonesty and lying

☐ misplaced priorities

F. What other concerns do you have about needs in the life of this congregation that you believe ought to be taken into consideration in planning for a year of preaching that will be appropriate and relevant?

_____

_____

_____

WORSHIP EVALUATION (SAMPLE)

Date of the service: _____

Theme of the service: _____

The following evaluation chart lists many parts of our worship life. The line indicates a continuum. Place an "x" on the line at the point that you feel best describes your experience of worship here. This exercise will help us identify both strengths and areas that need improvement.

Worship space

_____

Appropriate to the occasion   Inappropriate

Welcome to guests

_____

Warm and welcoming   Visitors ignored

Order of the service

_____

Easily understandable   Chaotic and hard to follow

Bulletin/worship sheet

_____

Well-prepared   Inaccurate or unclear

Announcements

_____

Fit into the service well   Distractions

Music

_____

Engaging and appropriate   Distraction from worship

Flow

_____

It all fit together   It seemed disjointed

Content of the service

Balance of the familiar and the fresh   Quite predictable

Congregational singing

Inspiring and uplifting   Dull and mumbling

Language

Easily understood   Religious jargon

Transitions

Each part moved smoothly   Seemed disjointed

Response

Called for a clear response   No response expected

WORSHIP EVALUATION (SAMPLE)

Date of service: _____

Theme of the service: _____

1. Did the worship service have a clear and unified theme? Express the theme as you sensed it in one sentence.
2. Did all the elements of the worship service relate to the theme? Give a few examples.
3. Were all the transitions smooth? Did the service flow well?
4. Was the worship God centered and Bible based?
5. Did the worship call for a response? State the clear application called for.
6. Was the environment positive and conducive to worship?
7. Was there a good balance between celebration and reflection? Give an example of each.
8. Walk through the service as though you were a visitor or guest. Identify the parts of the service that would be understandable to you. What do you think would be difficult to follow?
9. Did the service relate well to the needs of the worshipers? What needs were met?
10. Was the congregation fully involved in what was happening? In what ways?
11. Did the worship leaders seem sufficiently prepared to engage the other worshipers?
12. Evaluate the pace of worship—was it too fast, too slow, just right?

WORSHIP EVALUATION (SAMPLE)

Date of the service: _____

Theme of the service: _____

1. What words would you use to describe the overall impact of this worship service on you?
2. What in this worship service was particularly meaningful to you?
3. Which element(s) of this worship service best promoted a sense of the presence of God and fellowship with him?
4. Did each of the worship leaders make a positive contribution to the service? If not, what was distracting?
5. Did the service include a satisfactory balance between new and familiar material? If not, please explain.
6. Did anything in this worship service distract your attention from your conversation with God?
7. What should/could have been done differently?
8. Do you have any other suggestions based on your experience in this worship service?

General Evaluation of Our Worship Life

As you reflect upon our worship life over the past few months, write your overall impression as answers to the following questions.

1. List five terms that describe our worship life.
2. List four things you most appreciate about worship at this church.
3. What things in our worship services most need attention and change?
4. What is your vision for worship in this church 10 years from now?
5. What steps are necessary to bring about that vision?
6. What should be our primary focus during the next year?

RESOURCES FOR GROUP STUDY

Brink, Emily, ed. *Authentic Worship in a Changing Culture.* Grand Rapids: CRC Publications, 1997.

This resource was originally adopted and published by the Christian Reformed Church in 1997. It provides an excellent analysis of contemporary forces that affect worship, theological reflection about worship, and helpful questions to stimulate discussion.

Dawn, Marva. *How Shall We Worship? Biblical Guidelines for the Worship Wars.* Wheaton, Ill.: Tyndale House, 2003.

Dawn, a frequent writer on worship issues, organizes a study of worship issues around the words of Psalm 96, and in doing so finds good guidance for making worship decisions.

Evangelical Lutheran Church in America. *Principles for Worship.* Minneapolis: Augsburg Fortress, 2002.

Here's a book with solid principles for discussion. A commission of the ELCA has compiled 124 principles that reflect on aspects of worship. Each is amplified by additional documents and statements.

Furr, Gary A., and Milburn Price. *The Dialog of Worship: Creating Space for Revelation and Response.* Macon, Ga.: Smyth & Helwys, 1998.

This small book is an excellent tool to put in the hands of each committee member. It will further your discussions about how and where the dialogue of worship takes place—with God, within the community, in music, and in many settings.

Lathrop, Gordon. *What Are the Essentials of Christian Worship?* Minneapolis: Augsburg Fortress, 1994.

This booklet is one of a series in the "Open Questions in Worship" series from Augsburg Fortress. Lathrop, who teaches liturgy at the Lutheran Seminary in Philadelphia, sets out a series of essentials in an essay. Responses are included from Ruth Meyers (an Episcopal diocesan liturgist) and John Ferguson (who teaches organ and church music at St. Olaf College in Minnesota).

Long, Thomas G. *Beyond the Worship Wars: Building Vital and Faithful Worship*. Bethesda, Md.: Alban Institute, 2001.

After analyzing a variety of vital and faithful congregations, Presbyterian scholar Long provides nine marks of these churches that will help other churches in increasing their worship vitality.

Westermeyer, Paul. *The Heart of the Matter*. Chicago: GIA Publications, 2001.

This small book by a respected Lutheran pastor and musician will give a group excellent insights for discussing church music as praise, prayer, proclamation, and story, all as a gift from God.

APPENDIX B

WHEN YOU WORSHIP WITH US

We here provide the content of a booklet titled "When You Worship with Us—A User's Guide for Guests." This excellent and helpful booklet, intended for worship guests, provides them with a valuable informative tool.

WHEN YOU WORSHIP WITH US—A USER'S GUIDE FOR GUESTS

Dear Friend:

We are happy you have joined us for worship today.

This booklet is intended to help make your participation more meaningful. We hope it will give you a better understanding of what we do and why we do it. Take it home with you if you like.

Our warm welcome in Christ.

What's Going on Here?

Something very exciting indeed!

A worship service is a meeting between God and God's people. Each Sunday we come together as God's family in the presence of God.

Worship celebrates God's worthiness. In worship we experience this worthiness in a concentrated way. God's faithfulness inspires our faith; God's authority encourages our obedience; God's goodness stirs us to greater thankfulness; God's self-giving love nourishes our love and devotion. God's Spirit directs us to Jesus, our Savior and Lord, on whom our worship is centered.

In worship we also give to and receive from one another. The presence of people is absolutely essential. It is part of the reason we come together instead of merely watching a service on television or logging on to a computer. During the week we usually encounter God alone, or with a few friends or family members. Sunday worship provides a regular opportunity to do so as an entire congregation. It unites us more fully with Jesus Christ and with each other.

God's Action . . .

We worship at God's invitation, and in our worship it is God who takes the initiative. Worship services usually begin with a greeting from God, and they usually end with God's blessing. The words may be spoken by a minister or worship leader, but they are the words of God himself, recited or echoed from the Bible. The fact that God speaks to us so directly is one of the most astonishing things about worship.

God speaks whenever God's Word is read and proclaimed. Preaching is not just an expression of the minister's personal opinions. It is a form of holy communication in which the Holy Spirit brings the words of Scripture to life in our hearts. For this reason sermons always have a central place in our worship services.

God also speaks through baptism and the Lord's Supper. In these sacraments God's good news is affirmed in ways we can see, touch, and taste. The water used in baptism is a sign of the washing away of our sins and our new life in Christ; the bread and cup we share at the Lord's table are signs of Christ's sacrifice for us on the cross so that we might be accepted as children of God.

In most churches the furniture in the worship space includes a pulpit, a baptismal font, and a table used for the Lord's Supper—reminders that God speaks to us in both Word and sacraments.

. . . Our Action

Worship is an active dialogue in which God speaks and we respond with expressions of praise, confession, petition, and dedication. God invites us to be involved with and participate in worship. Worship is not a spectator sport; merely showing up is not enough.

Prayer is a vital part of our response to God. Through our prayers we offer praise for God's greatness, confess our sin, make known our own needs and those of the world, and give thanks for God's blessings.

Congregational worship is led by the minister or other designated persons usually called worship leaders or liturgists. Instrumentalists, choirs, or praise teams usually provide musical leadership. The real responsibility for worship, however, always rests with the congregation itself. Whether a worship leader prays on our behalf or a choir sings a prayer song or we recite a prayer in unison, we are all praying together. Worship leaders do not act instead of the congregation. They merely prompt us to participate with them. God hears those who pray silently as clearly as he hears those who are speaking aloud.

Timeless . . .

When we worship we are part of a fellowship of believers that spans the centuries. Congregational worship is a structured activity. The order of worship may be simple or complex, formal or informal; it may be "traditional" or "contemporary" in spirit; it may require a detailed printed text or none at all. At its core, however, it will draw on patterns and practices that have sustained believers since Bible times.

The basic elements of worship—prayers, singing, Scripture reading and preaching, offerings, and the celebration of the sacraments—are all mentioned and described in the Bible. Many of the actual words spoken during a service may come from the Bible itself. The service may include a statement of faith such as the Apostles' Creed, which Christians have been using for almost two thousand years. Sunday worship itself is an act that links us to the earliest New Testament believers, who set aside the first day of the week as the "Lord's Day" because it was the day on which Jesus rose from the grave.

Worship allows us to see beyond the limited horizons of our own experience. It unites us not only with an everlasting God but also with God's people in all times and places.

. . . Timely

Worship is never escapist. We always come to worship with our own here-and-now needs and concerns, and worship gives us fresh encouragement to manifest God's love in our everyday lives. Sermons apply timeless truths to contemporary situations. Prayers address the problems of the world and the specific joys and sorrows of worshipers. Often the service will include a time for announcements about important events in the life of the congregation.

Our offerings are also one way to participate in the work God is doing in the world. The church's deacons carefully account for our contributions and use them gladly to feed the hungry, educate children, give shelter to the homeless, and lead others to become followers of Jesus.

The offering is a vital act of worship, not a form of dues or admission fee. Our money is our time, our energy, and our lifeblood, minted into coin. By presenting in worship the firstfruits of our income, we show that God comes first in our lives. Our gift of money is a concrete response to the far greater gift God has given us in Jesus Christ. God's goodness demands a response not only in words but also in deeds. Cheerful and regular giving is one of the forms our discipleship can take.

Serious . . .

Worship can be a sobering experience. It brings us face to face with a just and holy God—and with the hard truth about our own sinfulness. It is not something to be done casually or thoughtlessly.

Because of the holiness of the God we worship, we want our minds and spirits cleansed anew in his presence. Sin is not something to celebrate, but neither can it be ignored. It must be confronted, confessed, and renounced. In the Scriptures we find countless examples of those who confess their sin, receive forgiveness in Christ, and then live in new gratitude and obedience. The flow of the worship service often reflects this biblical pattern of sin, salvation, and service.

Some who are worshiping today may still need to experience a first-time conversion from a life of unbelief. But even lifelong believers need to confess their sins regularly; each of us is still tempted away from the path of holiness. And as God's forgiven people we are called to remember all the suffering and injustice around us and to pray that God will make the broken places of the world whole again.

. . . Joyous

Authentic Christian worship always emphasizes the good news of God's grace: Although we are sinful, we have been made right with God in Christ.

As God speaks and as we respond in worship, our oneness with Christ grows more intimate. That is true cause for celebration!

Joy can be quiet as well as exuberant, but it is never far from the surface when God's people gather. That's one reason why music has always played such an important part in worship. Usually there will be music and singing from beginning to end of the service. Music before the service helps us put aside everyday thoughts and meditate on the majesty and goodness of God. Songs during the service enable everyone to participate in praising God and responding to God's Word. Music at the end of the service sends us away with gladness.

Many of our songs come directly from the Psalms of the Old Testament—the songbook of the first believing community—or from other passages of Scripture. To these we have added many other songs, new and old, that are biblical in content and centered on God. The choice of songs for a particular service depends on the theme of the service and the song's place in the order of worship.

Singing, like prayer, is the work of the entire congregation; in fact, singing itself can be a form of prayer. Whether you can sing well or not is unimportant. God wants everyone to celebrate.

What's Expected of Me?

The main thing we want you to know is that you are among friends. As God's family we enjoy celebrating with guests, and the God we serve welcomes you too. Jesus himself called his house a sanctuary for all people. There are no outsiders here, regardless of age, race, income, or education.

We hope it will be possible for you to participate fully. As you worship with us, you will not be embarrassed, tricked into something unexpected, or made to feel you don't belong. Don't worry about stumbling over something unfamiliar—no one will mind.

Understand that worship matters a great deal to us. We hope it will to you as well.

SELECTIVE AND ANNOTATED BIBLIOGRAPHY

Best, Harold M. *Music through the Eyes of Faith*. San Francisco: HarperSanFrancisco, 1993.

Explores the concepts of musical quality and excellence and aims for a better understanding of the connections between music making and the Christian faith.

Bradley, Randall. *From Postlude to Prelude: Music Ministry's Other Six Days*. Fenton, Mo.: Morning Star Music Publishers, 2004.

A comprehensive book on church music administration, designed for all who are involved in leading music ministries, to sharpen their skills and strengthen their ministries.

Bradner, John. *Symbols of Church Seasons & Days*. Wilton, Ct.: Morehouse-Barlow, 1977.

A helpful presentation and explanation of the symbols associated with each season of the Christian year.

Brink, Emily, ed. *Authentic Worship in a Changing Culture*. Grand Rapids: CRC Publications, 1997.

A resource adopted and published by the Christian Reformed Church. Includes an analysis of contemporary forces that affect worship, theological reflection about worship, and helpful questions to stimulate study and discussion.

Byars, Ronald. *The Future of Protestant Worship: Beyond the Worship Wars*. Louisville: Westminster John Knox Press, 2002.

An analysis of worship wars from a different perspective—the entrepreneurial spirit of today in a changed and changing culture. Historical comparisons and some projections about the paradigm of the future in worship.

Calvin Institute of Christian Worship. *The Worship Sourcebook*. Grand Rapids: Calvin Institute of Christian Worship, Faith Alive Christian Resources, and Baker Books, 2004.

A large compilation of teachings, readings, and prayers for each element of the worship service and each season of the church year. CD included.

Carson, Tim and Kathy. *So You're Thinking about Contemporary Worship*. St. Louis: Chalice Press, 1997.

A practical guide for developing contemporary worship services, based on the Carsons' experiences in their ministries.

Carson, Timothy C. *Transforming Worship*. St. Louis: Chalice Press, 2003.

An examination of how to worship authentically and an attempt to show how the ancient framework of Word and Table can come alive again in postmodern culture.

Dawn, Marva J. *How Shall We Worship?: Biblical Guidelines for the Worship Wars*. Vital Worship Series. Wheaton, Ill.: Tyndale House, 2003.

Reflections on Psalm 96 with a helpful study of worship issues around the words of the psalm, providing good guidance for making worship decisions.

————. *A Royal "Waste" of Time: The Splendor of Worshiping God and Being Church for the World*. Grand Rapids: Eerdmans, 1999.

An exploration of the splendor of worshiping God and being his church for the world, including such matters as our infinite center, community building, character formation, choices, and challenges.

————. *Reaching Out Without Dumbing Down: A Theology of Worship for This Urgent Time*. Grand Rapids: Eerdmans, 1995.

A theology of worship for the turn-of-the-century culture that examines the culture *surrounding* our worship, *of* our worship, *in* our worship, and worship *for the sake of* the culture.

Dearborn, Tim A., and Scott Coil, eds. *Worship at the Next Level: Insight form Contemporary Voices*. Grand Rapids: Baker Books, 2004.

A collection of 14 essays from diverse voices that provide insight on contemporary efforts to provide a well-rounded discussion on worship.

Evangelical Lutheran Church in America. *Principles for Worship*. Minneapolis: Augsburg Fortress, 2002.

A book with 124 principles for worship, compiled by a commission of the ELCA. Each principle is amplified by additional documents and statements.

Furr, Gary A., and Milburn Price. *The Dialog of Worship: Creating Space for Revelation and Response*. Macon, Ga.: Smyth & Helwys, 1998.

A tool for committee members to stir their discussions about how and where the dialogue of worship takes place—with God, within the community, in music, and in many settings.

Hawn, C. Michael. *One Bread, One Body: Exploring Cultural Diversity in Worship*. Vital Worship, Healthy Congregations series. Bethesda, Md.: Alban Institute, 2003.

A portrayal of how our worship is theologically formed yet also shaped by the emerging cultural circumstances of our society.

Lathrop, Gordon. *What Are the Essentials of Christian Worship?* Open Questions in Worship series. Minneapolis: Augsburg Fortress, 1994.

A small booklet that sets out a series of worship essentials in an essay, with responses from Ruth Meyers and John Ferguson.

Long, Thomas. *Beyond the Worship Wars: Building Vital and Faithful Worship*. Bethesda, Md.: Alban Institute, 2001.

An analysis of a variety of faithful congregations and an examination of nine marks of these congregations that will help other churches increase their worship vitality.

Mitman, F. Russell. *Worship in the Shape of Scripture*. Cleveland: Pilgrim Press, 2001.

A demonstration of how the structure common to the worship of most denominations is rooted in the Scriptures themselves, raising essential questions that each worship community should consider for the sake of faithful praise.

Old, Hughes Oliphant. *Worship: Reformed According to the Scripture.* Louisville: Westminster John Knox, 2002.

A classical historical study that summarizes the worship of Israel and the early church and traces the development of worship through the period of the Reformation and beyond.

Peterson, David. *Engaging with God: A Biblical Theology of Worship.* Downers Grove, Ill.: InterVarsity Press, 1992.

An attempt to get us behind the question of what style of worship we should use to understand the bedrock foundation for God's people—honoring him as he desires.

Plantinga, Cornelius, Jr., and Sue A. Rozeboom. *Discerning the Spirits: A Guide to Thinking about Christian Worship Today.* Grand Rapids: Eerdmans, 2003.

A book that grew out of a collaborative research team, engaging in dialogue about the spirits of our day and demonstrating the critical need for discernment in matters of worship.

Reformed Worship. Grand Rapids: CRC Publications.

A stimulating quarterly journal providing essays and resources for music, liturgy, and worship planning from a Reformed perspective.

Redman, Robb. *The Great Worship Awakening: Singing a New Song in the Postmodern Church.* San Francisco: Jossey-Bass, 2002.

An explanation of the ins and outs of worship trends, exploring four major developments—the "seeker service" movement, the "praise and worship" movement, the Christian worship music industry, and the liturgical renewal movement.

Schultze, Quentin J. *High-Tech Worship? Using Presentational Technologies Wisely.* Grand Rapids: Baker Books, 2004.

A thoughtful look at the use of technology in worship, giving practical guidance on how to use it, when to adopt or adapt, to help worshipers encounter God in fresh and meaningful ways.

Segler, Franklin M., and Randall Bradley. *Understanding, Preparing for, and Practicing Christian Worship.* Nashville: Broadman & Holman Publishers, 1996.

A comprehensive book that treats the foundations and meaning of worship, the means of expressing it, as well as the planning and conducting of worship.

Townley, Cathy. *Designing Worship Teams: Discovering and Birthing the Drama of Twenty-First-Century Worship.* Nashville: Abingdon, 2002.

Setting forth a new model for worship planning—the birthing of a team, functioning well and growing spiritually, through which the Holy Spirit can work.

Vann, Jane Rogers. *Gathered before God: Worship-Centered Church Renewal.* Louisville: Westminster John Knox, 2004.

Responses to the question of how churches can experience renewal through worship on the basis of a study of 10 small, medium, and large churches.

Webber, Robert E. *The Complete Library of Christian Worship.* Nashville: Star Song Publishing Group, 1993-1994.

A seven-volume work that provides countless resources for worship planning, short articles, and historical insight on worship practices in a wide variety of traditions.

———. *Planning Blended Worship: The Creative Mixture of Old and New.* Nashville: Abingdon, 1998.

A workbook with guidelines and instruction for each section of the fourfold pattern of the liturgy—the gathering, the word, the table, and the dismissal. Guides worship leaders in their planning, engaging them in reflecting on its meaning.

———. *Signs of Wonder: The Phenomenon of Convergence in Modern Liturgical and Charismatic Churches.* Nashville: Abbott-Martyn, 1992.

An analysis of how worship experiences today are bringing about a convergence of the historical and liturgical traditions.

————. *Worship Is a Verb: Eight Principles for Transforming Worship.* 2nd Edition. Peabody, Mass.: Hendrickson, 1992.

An examination of worship that offers creative and helpful suggestions for furthering the process of worship renewal. One of the first books on worship renewal that still speaks to today.

Westermeyer, Paul. *The Church Musician.* San Francisco: Harper & Row, 1988.

A practical handbook that gives insight into the role of musicians in worship.

————. *The Heart of the Matter.* Chicago: GIA Publications, 2001.

A small book to give groups excellent insights for discussing church music as praise, prayer, proclamation, and story, all as a gift from God.

Wetzler, Robert P., and Helen Huntington. *Seasons & Symbols: A Handbook on the Church Year.* Minneapolis: Augsburg Fortress, 1962.

A description of the symbols of the church year as a pageant of life unfolding in Christ.

Willimon, William H. *Worship as Pastoral Care.* Nashville: Abingdon, 1979.

Insights from pastoral care and pastoral psychology show how true pastoral care takes place within an active worshiping community of faith.

Witvliet, John D., ed. *A Child Shall Lead: Children in Worship.* Dallas: Choristers Guild; and Grand Rapids: Calvin Institute of Christian Worship, 1999.

A very helpful collection of essays and resources sure to be of great value to all who are committed to the inclusion of children in Christian worship.

————. *Worship Seeking Understanding: Windows into Christian Practice.* Grand Rapids: Baker Academic, 2003.

A wide range of issues in the worship of the church provide windows for examining the Christian practice of worship.

Wren, Brian. *Praying Twice: The Music and Words of Congregational Song.* Louisville: Westminster John Knox, 2000.

The significance and power of tune and text in congregational song explored from Wren's wide experience as theologian and hymnwriter.